Comments on other *Amazing Stories* from readers & reviewers

"Tightly written volumes filled with lots of wit and humour about famous and infamous Canadians."
Eric Shackleton, *The Globe and Mail*

"The heightened sense of drama and intrigue, combined with a good dose of human interest is what sets Amazing Stories *apart."*
Pamela Klaffke, *Calgary Herald*

"This is popular history as it should be... For this price, buy two and give one to a friend."
Terry Cook, a reader from Ottawa, on **Rebel Women**

"Glasner creates the moment of the explosion itself in graphic detail...she builds detail upon gruesome detail to create a convincingly authentic picture."
Peggy McKinnon, *The Sunday Herald*, on **The Halifax Explosion**

"It was wonderful...I found I could not put it down. I was sorry when it was completed."
Dorothy F. from Manitoba on **Marie-Anne Lagimodière**

"Stories are rich in description, and bristle with a clever, stylish realness."
Mark Weber, *Central Alberta Advisor*, on **Ghost Town Stories II**

"A compelling read. Bertin...has selected only the most intriguing tales, which she narrates with a wealth of detail."
Joyce Glasner, *New Brunswick Reader*, on **Strange Events**

"The resulting book is one readers will want to share with all the women in their lives."
Lynn Martel, *Rocky Mountain Outlook*, on **Women Explorers**

SHIPWRECKS OFF THE EAST COAST

AMAZING STORIES®

SHIPWRECKS OFF THE EAST COAST

Harrowing Tales of Rescue and Disaster

HISTORY

by Carmel Vivier

PUBLISHED BY ALTITUDE PUBLISHING CANADA LTD.
1500 Railway Avenue, Canmore, Alberta T1W 1P6
www.amazingstories.ca
1-800-957-6888

Extreme care has been taken to ensure that all information presented in
this book is accurate and up to date. Neither the author nor the
publisher can be held responsible for any errors.

Publisher	Stephen Hutchings
Associate Publisher	Kara Turner
Editor	Jill Foran
Digital Photo Colouring	Bryan Pezzi

We acknowledge the financial support of the Government
of Canada through the Book Publishing Industry Development
Program (BPIDP) for our publishing activities.

Altitude GreenTree Program
Altitude Publishing will plant twice as many trees as were used
in the manufacturing of this product.

Library and Archives Canada Cataloguing in Publication Data

Vivier, Carmel
Shipwrecks off the East Coast / Carmel Vivier.

(Amazing stories)
ISBN 1-55439-012-5

1. Shipwrecks--Atlantic Provinces. I. Title. II. Series: Amazing stories (Calgary, Alta.)

FC2019.S5V59 2005   910'.9163'44   C2005-903554-4

Printed and bound in Canada by Friesens
2 4 6 8 9 7 5 3 1

To my sons, André and Stefan,
for believing it could happen.

Contents

Prologue

Captain Reed watched in horror as more people threw themselves from the burning vessel. It was a terrible sight, made all the more surreal by the circus animals that were jumping in tandem with the panicked passengers. Horses and camels were being coaxed off the ship by their desperate handlers in the hopes they would swim to shore once they hit the water.

While each of the circus workers did their best to get the larger animals off the ship, there was one creature that couldn't be controlled. Mogul, the elephant, ran up and down the deck of the Royal Tar, *trumpeting in terror as the flames continued to engulf the vessel. From his position on the lifeboat, Captain Reed could hear the elephant's cries well above those of the passengers. Suddenly, the captain's eyes widened in dread as the elephant launched himself off the boat, aiming straight for a raft full of people below.*

Chapter 1
The *Arcana*

S ome ships, it seems, are simply fated to have problems. No matter who might own them, or who might sail them, misfortune and disaster just keep following these unfortunate vessels around. One such vessel was the *Arcana*, a three-masted schooner with a long history of bad luck.

Before she became the *Arcana*, this schooner was christened the *Jefferson Borden*, named after a prominent citizen of Fall River, Maine. Built in 1867 by David Clark of Kennebunk, Maine, she had a net tonnage of 533.39 and was 142 feet long. She was owned by her first commander, Captain Lemuel Hall, as well as several other shareholders, and claimed Boston as her homeport.

Scarcely three years after her launch, the *Jefferson*

Borden was caught in an exceptionally violent October gale that hammered the shipping lanes off the coast of Florida. Captain Hall tried to steer the ship to safety, but the storm had sprung up so quickly that he and the crew were trapped in the middle of it before realizing just how severe it was. Unable to escape the weather, they did their best to ride it out. They managed to release the deck cargo, hoping to lighten the ship's load, but the fierce wind and enormous waves soon damaged her rudder and tattered her sails, and there was little else the crew could do as the storm drove them closer and closer to the shoreline.

Captain Hall and his men braced themselves for the impact as the *Jefferson Borden* was swept through the crashing surf and slammed against the shore. A horrible tearing sound could be heard above the roar of the storm as the ship's hull was ripped open, spilling part of her remaining cargo into the sea.

Surveying his severely damaged vessel, Captain Hall knew he'd been lucky to make it to shore with only a few crew members injured. A short distance down the coast from where the *Jefferson Borden* lay stranded, the captain could see another ship, also grounded and laying completely on her side. As it turned out, 11 other ships were run aground in the vicious storm. The Florida coastline was strewn for over 80 kilometres with wrecked vessels, lost cargo, and debris.

After the *Jefferson Borden*'s beaching, her hull was auctioned off for $50 to the Tift brothers, Asa and Charles, of the

Florida Keys. The brothers then scraped together enough money to fix and recondition the schooner, but they quickly realized that in order to finance their new business venture, they would have to take on partners. Soon, Captain William M. Patterson from Edgecomb, Maine, bought up half the ship's shares, while George E. Towne of Boston purchased a quarter. This left the Tift brothers with only a quarter interest in the vessel.

Back at the *Jefferson Borden*'s homeport of Boston, Captain Patterson put together a new crew for the schooner. He recruited his brother, Corydon Trask Patterson, as first mate, and his cousin, Charles Patterson, as second mate. Soon after the crew was assembled, the owners obtained shipping contracts to carry cargo from Boston and New Orleans to London, England.

In late March 1875, five years after her refitting, the *Jefferson Borden* was on one of her regular voyages to London from New Orleans, her hold packed with a cargo of cotton-seed oil cake, when the black cloud of disaster struck again. The schooner, overloaded and short one crew member, ran into a bad storm. As violent winds came from all directions and the waters churned ferociously, the *Jefferson Borden* was helplessly tossed about, swamped by rogue waves crashing over her deck. The weather was so heavy that the casks lashed to the deck — and holding the crew's only drinking water — were at times submerged in the sea.

Just as they managed to sail out of the storm, and just

when the crew figured nothing else could go wrong, more bad luck struck: the ship sprung a leak. This meant that someone had to man the pump at all times, leaving crew members standing duty for up to 36 hours straight.

The long hours and tense atmosphere instigated a rumbling of discontent among the men. They were tired and frustrated. Lack of sleep, small food rations, and tainted drinking water made them an unpredictable bunch. When one of the crew, Ephraim Clark, refused a direct order from Captain Patterson to empty the water casks and help clean up the debris on the deck, the captain reached his limit of patience and punished Clark for insubordination. Clark, who had been a troublemaker from the very start of the voyage, persuaded two of the other crew members, George Millar and John Glew, to help him take over the ship in retaliation.

At midnight on April 20, the small group took action. It was the second mate's watch, which meant both the first mate and the captain would be in their quarters and were unlikely to interfere. Clark cut the schooner's foresheet, creating a problem that would require immediate attention. As Second Mate Charles Patterson approached the sail, Clark and Millar hit him from behind with a piece of block tackle and threw him overboard.

Meanwhile, First Mate Corydon Patterson was having a hard time sleeping and decided to join his cousin for a smoke. Shortly before 1 a.m., as Corydon Patterson stood asking Millar where his cousin had gone, he was attacked by

Clark from behind. With several swift stabs from a marline-spike, Clark killed the first mate and, with help from Glew, hurled his body into the sea.

Approximately one hour later, Captain Patterson left his quarters. He had made it a habit to take a walk and check on his ship each night around 2:30 a.m. Though he trusted his officers implicitly, he wasn't so sure about his crew — their lack of discipline made him anxious. The captain had the added burden of having his wife, Emma, on board for this particular voyage, and concern for her safety made him extra cautious.

As he set out on his customary walk, Captain Patterson quickly discovered that both his cousin and his brother were missing. Sensing something was terribly wrong, he quietly slipped back to his quarters, woke Emma, and ordered her to get dressed and be ready for anything. Then, going out on the deck again, he called forward to the crew, asking the whereabouts of the missing officers. Millar tried to trick the captain into going to the bow of the vessel, but Emma, being very intuitive, cautioned her husband to stay close by.

The captain wasn't sure what was going on, but suspected that, with both his brother and cousin missing, his command of the ship was in jeopardy. It appeared that Clark, Millar, and Glew were attempting a mutiny, and he needed to get control of the situation quickly. Finding someone other than his wife whom he could trust was his next plan of action. That someone was the steward, Albert Aiken. When awakened by Captain Patterson, Aiken quickly showed his loyalty by arming himself and the captain with revolvers and setting aside a double-barreled shotgun as a weapon of last resort.

Captain Patterson ordered the three rebellious crew members to surrender, but they ignored him. As the captain and steward crept forward from the cabin area, they were bombarded with pieces of broken grindstone, bits of iron, and anything else the mutineers could lay their hands on. Once again, Patterson called on the trio to surrender. Instead, the men threw more debris at the advancing pair and then retreated to the forecastle once their small supply of ammunition was used up.

The lull in fighting allowed Patterson to get closer and, before the men were even aware of what was happening, he and Aiken had thrown boards over the door to the forecastle and nailed it shut. For the third time, the captain ordered the men to give themselves up, and once again they refused. Patterson and Aiken then poured hot water down the forecastle's smoke-hole funnel and fired shots into the structure. This time, when the men were ordered to surrender, Millar staggered to the window and thrust out his hands. He was soon followed by Clark and Glew.

Once the rebels were locked away, the captain went to inspect his ship and track down his still-missing brother and cousin. But instead of finding them, he found the ship's cabin boy bound and gagged in the lazaretto — the mutineers had planned to make the young man steer the ship once they'd disposed of the captain, his wife, and any crew who did not fall in with them.

With the mutiny over, Captain Patterson found himself without a first or second mate. He'd lost two family members in the incident, and had no hope of recovering their bodies for burial. Worse still, the *Jefferson Borden* was approximately 1900 kilometres from the nearest port, and Patterson had only his wife, the steward, and the ship's boy on whose loyalty he could depend.

Getting back on course, the captain hailed the first vessel he saw, a Danish barque that sent a crew member over to help with the schooner. Things were more under control with the added crew member, and the *Jefferson Borden* made port in England in early May. The three rebels were placed in custody and sent to Boston in early July aboard the steamship *Batavia* to stand trial for mutiny.

Not long after the uprising, the owners of the *Jefferson Borden* tried to sell the schooner, but were unable to get rid of her. Undoubtedly discouraged, they may have thought that renaming the vessel would help put an end to her run of bad luck. Or perhaps they figured a new name would make her more appealing to prospective buyers. Whatever their reason, the *Jefferson Borden* became the *Arcana*.

Although he and the other owners were unable to sell the *Arcana*, Captain Patterson had no desire to continue captaining the ship. He found other captains for the job, and for several years after the mutiny, the *Arcana* continued to transport cottonseed oil cake to London. Then her owners managed to get her cargo route changed and she worked the trade routes to the West Indies, transporting lumber from Nova Scotia and New Brunswick.

In mid January 1885, with the new shipping year just starting, Captain Charles Holmes was looking for more crew members as the *Arcana* lay tied up at the Portland, Maine, harbour. Among the men he recruited was Patrick Lyons of St. Stephen, New Brunswick. Lyons was eager to get to work. It had been a while since he'd had a steady job, and he felt fortunate to have been chosen as a crew member aboard the schooner.

Two days after Lyons signed on, the *Arcana*, carrying Captain Holmes and 10 crew members, shipped out of Portland and headed up the Bay of Fundy toward Bear River, Nova Scotia, in the Annapolis Valley. The *Arcana* was in ballast for the trip to Bear River, where she would pick up a shipment of lumber bound for the West Indies. From Bear River, she would sail back down the Bay of Fundy to join the shipping lanes heading to the tropics.

Situated between New Brunswick and Nova Scotia, the Bay of Fundy boasts the highest tides in the world, and is also known as one of the East Coast's most treacherous bodies of water. Over the centuries, tidal surges and fast running water have carved the bay's shorelines and created many hidden rock formations, submerged ledges, and islands.

One of the more dangerous spots on the New Brunswick

side of the Bay of Fundy is an area known as Quaco Reef. Just offshore from the village of St. Martins, this reef runs out from Quaco Head on the west side of the harbour in a southeasterly direction for nearly two kilometres. For the most part, the reef lies hidden just below the water's surface during high tide. However, one small portion remains unsubmerged, and up until 1880, a lighthouse and a fog bell were located there. After a fire destroyed the lighthouse in 1880, the government decided that a new lighthouse would be built at Quaco Head, on the mainland. By 1885, the only visible reminder of the original lighthouse was a portion of the wharf and part of the foundation of the building itself, sitting on the reef.

As the *Arcana* headed into the Bay of Fundy, a vicious winter storm caught the vessel near Grand Manan Island, and Patrick Lyons was no longer sure he'd been lucky in getting his job. The pilot they'd hired on in Portland to guide them up and down the bay told Captain Holmes to stay on the north side of Grand Manan in order to find shelter from the storm.

Hugging the coastline as close as he dared, Captain Holmes navigated the *Arcana* farther up the bay, while desperately seeking protection in and around the area's many islands. For five or six days, the ship, battered by the storm, tried to ride out the winter gale using these anchorages. Finally, on January 25, they left the shelter offered by Grindstone Island at the head of the bay. But as they made their way down to Bear River, they encountered more nasty weather. The howling of the winds and whiteout conditions were nerve-wracking, and Lyons was beginning to think the terrifying storm would never end.

For the crew, staying dry was a constant challenge, and frostbite became a real threat as they tried to stand watch and keep the sails reefed in. The deck of the ship was slippery with ice, and navigating around it while keeping an eye on the sails was a dangerous job. More than once Lyons found himself almost slipping off the vessel due to the icy deck.

By January 28, conditions still had not improved, and the men were growing even more discouraged. Then, at around two o'clock that afternoon, Lyons thought he heard a fog whistle. Captain Holmes, as well as the pilot and some of the other crew members, also heard the sound. Though the raging blizzard kept them from visually identifying their whereabouts, the group concluded that the whistle had to be coming from the Cape Enrage light, just east of Alma, New Brunswick. As they readied the sails to duck into the harbour at Alma, the men were relieved they would have a safe harbour that night.

Unfortunately for the *Arcana* and her crew, they were farther down the bay than they'd anticipated. Between the winter storm and the fast running tides, Captain Holmes and his pilot, unable to take sightings from land, had miscalculated their position by almost 40 nautical miles. Instead of being near Alma, they were just southwest of St. Martins.

The orders had come to shorten the sails and the crew

had barely accomplished the task when they saw the lighthouse and land. Almost immediately, the vessel went broadside and hit Quaco Reef. It was 2:30 p.m., but it might as well have been midnight. The whiteout conditions and howling wind made visibility very poor, and only the light shining from the lighthouse at Quaco Head gave any indication as to where they were.

Some of the crew, including Lyons, took the time to change into drier clothing before trying to leave the damaged ship. Impatient to escape, Lyons then climbed the topmast rigging and, after a few failed attempts, managed to swing himself out onto the highest point of the reef, where the old lighthouse had once stood. The ship's second mate, O'Neill, tried to follow him, but he lost his grip on the ice-covered wood, fell under the bilge of the vessel, and broke his leg. Lyons quickly grabbed O'Neill and pulled him higher on the rocks, out of the water's reach. Then Lyons called out to the remaining crew on board the *Arcana*, instructing them to throw him a rope so he could help them ashore. He received no response.

Lyons knew he had to act. He could see the lighthouse to the west, and although he was afraid to leave O'Neill, who was badly injured, Lyons decided he would try to get help for the crew. Wet and cold, he stumbled along the reef through the blinding snow, plodding toward the lighthouse that stood on the hill, high above the site of the wreck.

When Lyons finally made it, the lighthouse keeper, Mr. Brown, sent him to fetch help some three kilometres away, promising that, in the meantime, he would retrieve O'Neill and any others who might have made it to the reef. According to Brown's later court statement, he went alone to the wreck at around 4 p.m., taking a lifebuoy and a line. Calling out to the vessel, he got no response from the crew, and although he searched, he couldn't find anyone — not even O'Neill — on the reef. Worried that he'd be cut off by the rising tide if he spent any more time looking for survivors, Brown hurried back across the race (the spit of land connecting the reef to the mainland).

While Brown was searching the reef, Patrick Lyons managed to get help in the form of the lighthouse keeper's brother. However, by the time the pair arrived back at the lighthouse, the race was covered by the tide. Anxious to reach the crew, Lyons tried to talk Brown and his brother into taking a boat across to the reef, but Brown thought this plan was too dangerous. Besides, he pointed out to Lyons, he'd already been to the reef and hadn't been able to find anyone.

Lyons, exhausted from the shipwreck and his struggle through the snowstorm, was finally persuaded to go to bed. While he slumbered soundly, Brown had a more restless sleep. Several times during the night, the lighthouse keeper was awoken by shouts coming from the reef — calls for help from crew members stranded on the rocks. Despite hearing the desperate pleas, he refused to risk taking a boat over the race with the heavy sea crashing against the rocks.

The next morning, as soon as it was light and the tide

was low enough, Lyons, Brown, and his brother managed to get over the race to the reef, where they found three members of the crew — First Mate Stephen Siteman, a Danish crewman known only as Peter, and a third crewman named Louis Gain — all frozen to death. The second mate, O'Neill, was not among the three, and it was assumed he'd lost his grip on the icy rocks or was washed away by the tide. Lyons and his companions transported the bodies to the mainland and placed them in a small shed adjacent to the lighthouse, where they remained until claimed by family members.

Once the storm had abated and the people of St. Martins got word of the shipwreck, search parties were sent out along the shore to look for the rest of crew. But the searchers found only two more bodies — a French crew member named Charley and the ship's pilot from Portland.

Of the 11 people that had departed Maine for Nova Scotia aboard the *Arcana* on that fateful trip, only one person survived — Patrick Lyons. Five bodies were recovered, but there were no signs of the captain and the rest of the crew.

Soon after the tragedy, a coroner's inquest was convened by Dr. Gillmore, the attending physician from Saint John. A jury soon rendered the following verdict: "We, the coroner's jury, in the case of the five men of the schooner *Arcana*, on the 29th of January, 1885, have arrived at the conclusion that two of the men, the pilot and Charley the Frenchman, came to their death by drowning and that three of them, the first mate, Peter the Dane and Louis Gain, came to their death from exposure while on the old lighthouse wharf. We recommend that some shelter be provided on said wharf for like emergencies, and we consider that the accident is altogether attributable to the want of a steam whistle in connexion with the present light."

The verdict of "death by exposure" sent outrage through the community and created more questions than answers. Not surprisingly, there was much contention and controversy over the lighthouse keeper's actions. People in the area were suspicious of Brown's story. They demanded to know why he had sent Patrick Lyons for help instead of taking him back to the reef to search for survivors. They also began to question if Brown had gone to the wreck at all that day.

When interviewed by a reporter, Captain A. J. Siteman, brother to the deceased first mate of the *Arcana*, admitted he thought it strange that Brown had not attempted to get a boat over to the stranded crew members when he'd heard their cries for help "for the greater part of the night." Siteman also found it strange that a lighthouse situated near such a dangerous piece of water was not equipped with a rocket and line. With such a device, his brother and any others who had made it to the reef might have been rescued from the shore without a boat ever having to enter the water.

There was also some question as to what might have caused Patrick Lyons and the other crew members of the *Arcana* to think they'd heard a foghorn or whistle. While Cape Enrage did have a foghorn whistle, there was no foghorn at

Quaco Head at that time. Was it the sound of the wind blowing offshore that had caused them to alter their course and end up wrecked on the ledges at Quaco Head?

These questions remained unanswered, and soon the job of claiming the bodies took precedence over the many unsolved mysteries surrounding the tragedy. Captain Siteman had travelled from Halifax to claim his brother's body. The first mate's burial was to be in Halifax, where he'd resided with his wife and children before moving to Portland to take up his position with Captain Holmes aboard the *Arcana*. Two other bodies, that of the pilot and another not named, were readied for shipment by train to Portland, where both deceased had family and friends waiting to take them to their final resting places.

The remaining two bodies were not claimed. Rather than place them in a pauper's grave, the people of St. Martins and Quaco decided to give them a decent burial. The story of the crew dying from exposure so close to the shore touched the hearts of the local fishermen and shipbuilders, and their families, and they could not bear the thought of these two men lying in an unrecognized grave, far from their homes and loved ones. Instead, the bodies were taken to the Temperance Hall in St. Martins, where they were prepared for burial and placed in fine caskets — the best that could be found in the village. The deceased were then given a burial ceremony by the Church of England and laid to rest in the Episcopal cemetery in West Quaco. Eventually, a memorial headstone was placed on the grave in remembrance of the sailors who had lost their lives aboard the *Arcana*.

The jury recommendation that a shelter be built on the site of the old lighthouse was not heeded. Although there were letters of support and petitions signed by merchants and shippers alike, it took two more years before a foghorn was finally installed at Quaco Head.

When a reporter asked Captain A. J. Siteman what he thought of the present location of the Quaco Head light, he responded, "In my opinion it was better where it was than on the present site. Had it been on the reef the men would have had some place to go instead of freezing to death with the light from the lamp on shore shining in their faces. It is a hard death for a man to perish with the cold within sight of a lighthouse."

Chapter 2
The SS *Atlantic*

he year was 1873, and the Hindley family was moving to America. Tired of the low-paying jobs in South Lancashire, and worried about his sons' futures, Patrick Hindley was ready to leave England and take his chances in the New World. His wife, Mary, was torn about leaving her friends behind, but her married daughters were in America, and she was looking forward to reuniting with them and their families.

Patrick and Mary's oldest son, Michael, was also eager to leave. The 18-year-old worked in the cotton mill alongside his father, and he wanted something more, something better than living in a heavily industrialized city and working long hours for little pay. Michael had heard that there was work for an honest man in America, and a decent wage to go along with it.

The SS Atlantic

Perhaps the most eager of all the Hindleys was the youngest member of the family, 10-year-old John. The idea of travelling across the ocean on a big steamship was thrilling to the boy. He listened to his parents and older brother talking about the trip and imagined the great adventures he would have, both aboard the ship and in his new home. As the family's day of departure — March 20, 1873 — grew closer, young John could barely contain his excitement. He knew his trip to New York City on the SS *Atlantic* would be unforgettable.

The White Star Line was proud of its modern steamships, and the SS *Atlantic* was indeed something to be proud of. Built in Belfast, Ireland, by Harland & Wolfe in 1871, this 3700-ton liner made her first voyage from New York to Liverpool in just 10 days. She was one of the best-designed passenger ships of her time, with three masts, one funnel, six watertight bulkheads, and four engines. All of this, plus her first-rate steering mechanisms, made her a valuable asset to the Oceanic Steam Navigation Company, who owned the White Star Line.

The *Atlantic* was built for general transatlantic trade and could accommodate up to 1200 passengers. On the trip departing from Liverpool for New York on March 20, she would be carrying 33 cabin passengers, another 794 people in the steerage section, and approximately 149 crew members.

The captain for the voyage was James Agnew Williams, a hard-working Welshman with a mercurial temperament and a knack for staying calm in troublesome situations.

The night before the *Atlantic* was to depart Liverpool, Captain Williams showed his chief officer, John W. Firth, their sailing orders. Williams had recently been forced by his superiors to "lay off the best crew in port in order to save a week's wages," and had ended up hiring the most unruly bunch of "tough guys" he'd ever seen. Now his orders were to combine safety and speed on this journey — it was a boost to a steamship company's reputation if its ships arrived ahead of schedule.

What distressed Williams the most this particular evening, however, was the matter of coal. When he asked Firth how much Welsh coal had been loaded aboard, he was told it wasn't all Welsh, but that they also had about 100 tons of English coal on the ship. Both Williams and Firth considered English coal useless because it didn't burn well — the crew would have to burn twice as much of it in order to produce enough heat for the boilers.

The next morning, as the *Atlantic*'s crew prepared for departure and passengers boarded the ship, 10-year-old John Hindley could barely contain his excitement. It didn't matter that the ship's steerage section, where he and his family were staying, was not as luxurious as first class — it was enough for the youngster that he was setting out on the journey of a lifetime.

John wasn't the only excited youngster on the *Atlantic*. Shortly after coming on board, he met up with a boy his own age — William Jones — who was also immigrating to America with his family. The two boys took an instant liking to each other, and as the ship's mooring lines were cast off and she moved out of Liverpool Harbour, the pair stood side by side, hanging on to the railing and watching England disappear from sight.

John and William became fast friends, and they spent much of their trip exploring the ship together. There were mysterious places to investigate all over the *Atlantic*, and the two boys inspected everything. They also made friends with Chief Officer Firth, who often took time to explain the workings of the vessel to them as he made his rounds.

There were other children on board the *Atlantic* as well, the majority of whom were steerage passengers travelling with their parents and siblings. Indeed, most of the passengers in steerage were making their way to America or Canada in search of a better way of life.

Meanwhile, the majority of passengers travelling in the ship's saloon section were Americans returning from holidays in Europe. There were also a number of first class passengers who were going back to America after having lived abroad for a number of years.

The time spent on the *Atlantic* was relaxing for most of the ship's saloon passengers. They ate in a resplendent dining room with the captain and officers and spent their evenings listening to music or discussing politics over drinks in one of the salons. In steerage, the passengers didn't have it quite as good. The accommodations were overcrowded and the bathroom facilities left a lot to be desired, but there was plenty of good food and no one went to bed hungry.

As the passengers on the *Atlantic* settled in for their long journey, Chief Officer Firth was growing increasingly concerned. Like Captain Williams, Firth found the ship's new crew to be lacking in discipline, and not nearly as attentive to their duties as the previous crew had been. Each time Firth made his rounds, he spotted loose ropes and pieces of gear out of place. And, on more than one occasion, he found himself reprimanding crew members for their negligence.

With each negative report from his chief officer, Captain Williams's concern about the crew deepened, too. He knew that the men were inexperienced, and that none of them seemed to care about their jobs. Unfortunately, there wasn't much he could do about the situation. He only hoped the crew's inexperience wouldn't put his ship or passengers in jeopardy.

After a brief stopover in Queenstown, Ireland, the *Atlantic* was on course for New York, but she met with a strong head wind early on in the journey. Continually steering the ship into the head wind, Captain Williams was unable to make use of her sails and instead had to rely entirely on the coal supply to keep her moving.

On March 31, just before noon, the captain and his officers stood on the bridge of the *Atlantic* and discussed their situation. The news wasn't good. They were over

600 kilometres from Sandy Hook (a lighthouse used as a reference point to guide ships into New York Harbour), and the coal supply was running very low. The stormy weather and head winds they'd encountered throughout the journey had used up more fuel than anticipated, and unless they picked up a favorable wind, they certainly wouldn't make it to Sandy Hook before the coal ran out. Captain Williams thought back to the conversation he'd had with Firth the night before they departed and realized he'd been right about the English coal — it had proven inadequate for this journey.

The captain had to decide whether or not to change course. There was insufficient fuel on board to complete the trip to New York, and without favourable winds they could not use their sails. With the barometer glass dropping steadily, he knew they were in for more bad weather and realized he had little choice but to order the crew to alter direction. They would now head for Halifax to wait out the storm and secure more coal before heading on to New York.

The fact that none of the officers of the *Atlantic* had ever brought a ship into Halifax Harbour did not bother them — they had charts covering the coastline, after all. And Halifax, being a port that was used widely for both passenger ships and freight vessels, had well-marked approaches.

By early morning on April 1, the *Atlantic* was well on her way to her new destination. Second Officer Henry Metcalf was manning her bridge for the middle watch, between midnight and 4 a.m., and had orders to wake the captain at 3 a.m.

Though a fine sleet was falling, the sky was not fully covered with cloud and there was no fog to hinder the duty watch.

Fourth Officer John Brown was also on watch, and he confided to Metcalf that he'd overheard the chief engineer say they were travelling faster than anticipated. With that news, Metcalf ordered another log line to measure the *Atlantic's* speed. Using the ship's automatic telegraph connection, Quartermaster Charles Raylance relayed the log line reading to Metcalf. Then, as Raylance made his way back to the bridge, an overwhelming feeling of dread washed over him. Standing astern, he noticed that the heavy seas were breaking just beyond the port side of the ship. The waves appeared to be hitting rocks or shoals hidden below the water's surface, and the *Atlantic* was heading straight for them.

Sailing at a full 12 knots, the *Atlantic* struck one of the many long reaches of rock that lay just below the waterline along the Nova Scotia coast. The ship was almost 16 kilometres southwest of where she should have been. The impact of the collision caused her bow to hang on the rocks while the wind and waves turned her sideways to port, slamming her against more rocks, which quickly tore gashes in her hull below the waterline.

The force of the impact was felt throughout the ship. People were knocked from their berths, and lifeboats were flung into the sea. Many of the passengers in the steerage section became trapped below, and as the ship took on more water, they drowned in their rooms. Those who did manage to escape their quarters drowned in the steerage hallways, which were crowded with desperate people unable to reach the hatchways leading to the upper decks.

Third Officer Cornelius Brady had been asleep in his quarters when the ship struck the rocks. When he finally managed to make his way to the deck, he discovered that the lifeboats on the port side had been lost, washed overboard by the waves. Brady quickly found an axe and used it to get one of the starboard lifeboats ready. As soon as the boat swung loose, a group of panicked passengers rushed toward it. Luckily, it reached the water before they could upset it. Brady managed to get two women into the lifeboat before a dozen men crowded in as well.

Turning his attention back to the activity on the *Atlantic* for a moment, Brady noticed that the captain and the other officers were having little success in launching the remaining lifeboats. Suddenly, the ship gave a shudder, and her gigantic boilers exploded. Brady watched in horror as the *Atlantic* fell over on her beam ends and sank, taking with her the lifeboat he had just launched. The people aboard the small vessel were too slow to respond and drowned as the ship pulled the lifeboat under.

With the hull of the *Atlantic* almost completely submerged, Captain Williams and his officers urged the passengers to move forward to the bow, put themselves into the rigging, and hold on. Soon, the ship's masts and rigging were dotted with people clinging to whatever they could grab.

Captain Williams managed to get one of the young saloon passengers, Lilian Davidson, into the rigging, but had less luck with the girl's mother. With the swaying of the deck, Lewiston Davidson, unable to keep her balance, was thrown into the sea. Williams then put Lilian in the care of Chief Officer Firth, commanding him to keep her safe.

Meanwhile, other passengers were doing whatever they could to stay alive. Patrick Leahy and William Hogan were among the many people who had boarded the *Atlantic* with plans to start fresh in America. When the ship first struck the rocks, both men had thrown on some clothing and headed for the deck. Although they managed to make it to their destination, their nightmare was far from over. The *Atlantic* soon went into a steep roll, and Leahy and Hogan raced for her port side, managing to grab some rigging just as a huge wave swept over the ship. Both men were soaked, but secure for the time being.

Unfortunately, their perch gave the pair a view that would haunt them forever. Glancing downward, Hogan saw what at first glimpse appeared to be a huge mass of seaweed being pushed forward and then swept back by the pounding of the waves against the rocks. He then heard a terrible moaning sound and looked down again. His second glimpse made him ill. The mass was not comprised of seaweed at all — it consisted of women and children being washed out through the holes in the ship's steerage section.

Young John Hindley was not among the steerage

passengers in the water. He'd been asleep when the ship hit the rocks, but the impact of the collision immediately woke him, throwing him from his bed. Not sure what was happening, John got up and followed some of the other passengers as they made their way out of the steerage section and onto the deck through a porthole. The deck was tilting badly, and the cold waves splashing over the ship made John wish he'd stayed below with his family.

Before he had a chance to return to them, however, people began grabbing him and passing him forward. He was finally passed to someone who tied him high in the ship's rigging so that he would not be washed overboard by the waves. Wet and cold, he held on to his perch, finally realizing that the *Atlantic* was sinking.

As John and countless others clung desperately to the ropes and chains of the doomed ship, several of the crew, under the leadership of Third Officer Brady, tried to get attention from potential rescuers by firing flares. When there was no response to these, the men decided they would attempt to rig a lifeline from the *Atlantic* to Marr's Head, a rocky island that lay 12 to 15 metres off the bow. Once the first line was secure, they would rig another line from the rocky island to the larger Meagher's Island, about 230 metres farther inland.

Brady and his small crew knew that in order to get the lifeline from the ship to Marr's Head, someone would have to swim through the frigid, pounding sea. Worse, the designated person would also have to swim among the partly hidden reefs and shoals, running a risk of being thrown into jagged rocks by the wild surf.

Quartermaster Edward Owen was the first to attempt the swim to the rocky island, but he was soon pulled back to the ship, half drowned and coughing up seawater. Quartermaster Robert Thomas went next, and he managed to get a line secured. Then, with the aid of Thomas's line, Quartermasters George Speakaman and William Purdy, carrying more ropes, made the swim to Marr's Head and fashioned a pulley system to get the passengers off the ship. The system consisted of several lines twisted together to make a hawser, or cable. Attached to the cable was a life ring through which the passengers would put their legs. A second and third rope were then used to pull the passengers along the cable to safety.

All through the night, Brady and his small crew worked to get as many people as possible off the ship. Braving the crashing waves and bobbing line, the passengers did their best to hang on to the life ring as they swayed above the water. At times they would find themselves completely immersed in the frigid surf, and the cold water and biting wind made many clumsy with hypothermia. The weakest of the group — the women, children, and elderly — sometimes lost their grip and were washed away before ever reaching Marr's Head. Still others succumbed to the cold on Marr's Head and did not have the strength to continue on to the larger island.

By daybreak, the men had managed to get another pulley system rigged and they moved as many passengers as possible over to Meagher's Island, one of several islands that sit to the southwest of the village of Lower Prospect. At that time, there was only one family inhabiting the island — the Clancies. Michael Clancy and his invalid wife were at home at the time of the wreck. Their 28-year-old daughter, Sarah Jane Clancy Riely, was also there, visiting and helping to look after her mother.

Once they were safely on Meagher's Island, Quartermaster Robert Thomas and a few passengers set out to see if they could get help. Spotting a light from the Clancy residence, they made their way to the house and knocked on the door. Soon the small home was overflowing with survivors. The Clancies led a very simple life, but what they had they shared with the passengers of the *Atlantic*. Everyone in the house was given dry clothing or a blanket and something hot to drink.

Sarah and her father then gathered more blankets, clothing, tea, and anything else they thought might be useful, and headed out into the cold April morning looking for survivors who were too weak to make it to their home. The scene they came upon was gruesome. The shoreline of their little island was strewn with bodies, some dead, most barely alive, collapsed from cold and exhaustion. Moving from person to person, Michael and Sarah quickly handed out their meagre supplies. Anyone who had strength left to walk was quickly shown the way back to the Clancy house for shelter.

Meanwhile, on nearby Ryan's Island, a small island tucked between Meagher's Island and Lower Prospect,

Edmund Ryan was preparing his summer home for the upcoming fishing season. As he worked, he happened to look out his window toward Meagher's Island and was sure he saw something moving. Thinking that Michael Clancy might be in trouble, he opened his front door to get a better look and was surprised to see people walking around the island.

Grabbing his coat, Ryan rushed outside to find out what was going on. Not far from his doorway, he came across a sailor, half conscious, lying among the rocks. Ryan quickly carried the stranger back to the house. When the sailor was fully cognizant, he identified himself as Quartermaster Robert Thomas and told Ryan about the shipwreck. He also explained that survivors from the wreck were being cared for at the Clancy home. Ryan quickly pulled on his coat, jumped into his small fishing dory, and headed across the channel to get help from his brothers and the other fishermen of Lower Prospect.

When word of the disaster reached Lower Prospect, the people of the tiny fishing village sent a runner to Terence Bay, a nearby community, to get more help. Then the village men readied their fishing vessels and went to assist in the rescue. The small fishing boats struggled through the breakers to reach the passengers and crew still stranded on the sinking ship, but most had to turn back because of the pounding surf. One vessel capsized, and the crew on board, exhausted from their efforts, swam to shore.

Next, a few larger fishing boats made their way out to the wreck. Risking their lives and straining over the oars, the fishermen managed to unload most of the remaining passengers as they made trip after trip from the safety of Lower Prospect to the sinking vessel.

Captain Williams, who had tied himself into the ship's rigging after helping countless others do the same, watched from his perch with bated breath as the fishing boats struggled to rescue his passengers. Meanwhile, back onshore, Third Officer Brady was looking for the captain among the survivors and was soon informed that Williams was still on the ship. In no time, Brady, along with Quartermasters Raylance and Speakaman, had talked their way onto one of the fishing boats and were headed out to the wreck in the hope of rescuing their captain.

But Captain Williams's strength was fading fast. His legs, which he'd injured badly earlier in his career, had lost all feeling. When Brady finally made it to the *Atlantic* and called for the captain to jump from the rigging, Williams told him he couldn't move his legs.

Higher up in the rigging, two saloon passengers — S.W. Vick from North Carolina and Simeon Camachio from New York — saw the captain's predicament and carefully made their way down to him. Using the rope Williams had used earlier to tie himself to the rigging, they carefully lowered his half-frozen body into the waiting boat and then jumped in after him.

By that time, the crew of the fishing boat that Third

Officer Brady was commanding was growing tired. From what they could tell, there were only three people left on board the *Atlantic* who were still alive: Chief Officer Firth, Lilian Davidson (the girl who had been left in Firth's care), and 10-year-old John Hindley. All three were positioned very high up in the rigging.

Making another pass to the ship, Brady called for Firth to jump to the fishing boat, but Firth refused. Instead, at Firth's urging, John Hindley untied the rope that was holding him to the rigging and made a wild jump for Brady's boat. He missed the target and hit the water, but one of the strong fishermen reached over the side of the boat and grabbed him from the waves.

After taking a final look at Firth and the young girl in the rigging, Brady headed to shore with his latest survivor. Exhausted, and unable to get a crew to go out to the wreck one last time, he followed his captain's orders to go immediately to Halifax and get word to the London office about the shipwreck.

As Brady headed to Halifax, the Anglican minister in Terence Bay, Reverend William Johnson Ancient, attempted to galvanize the rescuers. He wasn't ready to give up on the *Atlantic*'s two remaining passengers. Finally, he persuaded a group of men to make one last rescue attempt, and he agreed to lead them. The reverend had spent his early years serving in the Royal Navy in England and had considerable experience around ships.

Soon, one last rowboat was heading out to the scene. Putting his own life at great risk, Reverend Ancient boarded the *Atlantic* to assist Firth and the young woman. As he neared the pair, the reverend could see that the young woman was dead, her frozen body held closely by Firth, who was almost dead himself. For six long hours, he had stubbornly held on to both Lilian and the rigging, hoping for help. But now, with rescue so near, he couldn't get his frozen fingers to let go of the ropes.

Reverend Ancient tied a spare rope around Firth's waist as a lifeline. Then, just as he managed to pry open Firth's frozen fingers, an enormous wave came crashing upwards, sweeping Firth, and the body of Lilian Davidson, clear of the rigging and into the sea. Luckily, the lifeline held. With great skill and strength, the reverend maneuvered Firth into the rowboat and then managed get himself into the boat as well. The fishermen manning the oars rowed both men to the safety of Meagher's Island.

When John Hindley was brought to shore, Sarah Clancy Riely was overcome with grief for the young boy. She watched as John looked around for his family and did not see them. He also looked for his friend, William Jones, but couldn't find him, either. Sarah had known from listening to the rescuers that most of the families in the steerage section of the ship had not made it. She knew that the young boy's family had probably perished in the shipwreck, and her heart went out to him. Gathering a dazed John in her arms, she took him to her father's home, where she made sure he was given dry clothing and food.

When word of the shipwreck finally reached Halifax, more ships were sent out to take the survivors to the city. The rescue efforts had greatly stretched the limits of the households in Terence Bay and Lower Prospect, where warm blankets and food supplies were running low. With over 400 survivors to feed and clothe, most families from the small fishing villages shared what they had, but it was hardly enough. Moreover, many of the survivors, suffering from frostbite, hypothermia, broken bones, and other serious injuries, needed extensive medical attention. Once in Halifax, they could get the care they needed and would also be able to book passage on to New York.

On April 18, 1873, the Court of Inquiry met in Halifax to pass judgment on the wreck of the *Atlantic* and the loss of life that ensued. The tribunal found that Captain Williams was justified in changing his course to head for Halifax when he knew he did not have enough coal on board to reach New York. He was, however, found responsible for not keeping a closer watch on his crew, and for not making sure that regular soundings were taken. The tribunal also found that the officers on duty at the time the ship ran aground were at fault for not keeping a better watch in unfamiliar waters, and for failing to wake the captain as requested. The judgment brought down saw Captain Williams's extra master and master certificates suspended for two years.

The *Atlantic*'s cargo, which was valued at around half a million dollars, was made up mostly of hardware, earthenware, and dry goods. There was also about $25,000 worth of machinery bound for the mills of Fall River, Massachusetts. All was lost.

John Hindley's sisters, who both lived in Newark, New Jersey, brought their brother home to live with them, but not before several attempts were made to adopt the lone surviving child of the shipwreck. The White Star Line made one adoption attempt, offering to school young John and train him for work with their company. Another offer came from an alderman in New York, and there was a rumour that P. T. Barnum of Barnum and Bailey's Circus offered $20,000 — quite a sum in 1873 — for the privilege of selling John Hindley's photograph. John's sisters, however, insisted on raising him with their own children in Newark with a view to letting him lead as normal a life as possible after the shipwreck.

There were 975 passengers and crew on board the SS *Atlantic* when she ran aground near Marr's Head, Nova Scotia, on that fateful April Fool's morning. Of the people on board, 562 lost their lives. Every woman and child except one — John Hindley — were lost.

Today, two burial spots near the sight of the wreck hold some of those unfortunate souls who perished that day — 277 passengers are buried in the churchyard at Sandy Cove, on Terence Bay, and another 150 are buried in the cemetery across the road from the Star of the Sea Church in Lower Prospect.

Chapter 3
The *Fairy Queen*

I t was October 5, 1853, and excitement was in the air at the Young household in Charlottetown, Prince Edward Island. The Honourable Charles Young's oldest niece, Arabella DeWolfe, was about to leave for England to start a new life as the wife of a clergyman. A year earlier, the Reverend Mr. Macnair had been posted on Prince Edward Island, where he'd met and fallen in love with Arabella. Upon being recalled to England, he proposed to the young woman, and to his delight, she accepted.

Now Arabella was getting ready to say her final farewells to her family. It was a bittersweet parting because she would be leaving her beloved younger sister, Alice, behind. As she looked around at the luggage piled up in the bedroom, Arabella wondered if she would ever see her sister again.

England was far away, and with Alice's own engagement to a man in Nova Scotia, it seemed doubtful.

At least she wouldn't have to say goodbye to her sister right away; arrangements had been made for Alice and her maid, Jane, to accompany Arabella on the first leg of her journey. The threesome would travel aboard the *Fairy Queen*, a steamer that carried mail and passengers between Charlottetown and Pictou, Nova Scotia. From Pictou, they would journey on to Halifax, where Arabella would leave her companions and board the Cunard Line steamer *America* for her trip to England.

Arabella marvelled at how she could feel so excited and yet so nervous about her trip at the same time. Perhaps it was the brewing storm, which was moaning around the windows and doors of her uncle's house, that was unsettling her. Or perhaps it was her upcoming wedding that had her jumping at every shadow. Whatever was causing her to be so anxious, Arabella tried to keep it from interfering with the short time she had left to spend with her family.

On the morning of October 7, the storm that had worried Arabella the night before was still raging. Rain squalls and a strong northwest wind were making travel unfavourable along the Northumberland Strait (the stretch of water between Prince Edward Island and mainland Nova Scotia). The captain of the *Fairy Queen*, William Belyea, decided to delay the steamer's 6 a.m. departure, hoping that the wait would allow for a break in the weather.

By noon, the seas were calm enough, and Captain Belyea began to round up his crew. Unfortunately, several of the crewmen had decided to wait out their extended stay in Charlottetown at one of the local taverns. As a result, some were in no shape to work, and two were left behind completely. It was not an auspicious start to the journey.

The *Fairy Queen* had 13 passengers and 13 crew on board when she finally departed Charlottetown's Pontal Wharf. Just as the steamer was leaving, one of the passengers, Henry Pineo Jr. from Pugwash, Nova Scotia, noticed that there was water on the floor of the passenger cabin. When he questioned a crew member about this, he was told the water would disappear once they got underway.

Meanwhile, Arabella, Alice, and Jane settled in for the voyage. Wanting to spend as much time with each other as possible, they sat slightly apart from the other passengers and began to chat. The sisters were not impressed with the condition of the passenger cabin, and from the snatches of conversation they overheard, their fellow travellers weren't too happy, either.

As the ship passed through Hillsborough Bay, a protected body of water not too far out from Charlottetown, everything appeared to be going smoothly. When she moved into more open water just past Point Prim, however, the Northumberland Strait was far from calm. Waves threatened the steamer, and it wasn't long before they were washing over her deck, causing the gangway hatch to break open and bringing about some other minor damage. For the next five hours, the *Fairy Queen* slowly and steadily made her way across the strait, struggling to stay on course through the menacing sea.

At around 5:30 p.m., it became apparent that the steamer was in trouble. The passengers were all in the cabin below deck when word came down that the main tiller rope (the principal steering mechanism for the vessel) had snapped, and that the Northumberland Strait had turned into a raging sea, churned up by the strong northwest winds. The breaking of the tiller rope caused the ship to "broach to," or go sideways into a huge wave, and the vessel was deluged again.

Most of the male passengers grabbed their coats and went topside to assist in fixing the tiller rope. They held the tiller rope tight while the first mate and some of the crew attempted to splice it together. At first the group thought they'd succeeded, but it soon became apparent that the knot was too far forward and would not allow the wheel to work properly. The knot was quickly undone and retied again, this time in the proper place.

Though the tiller rope was now repaired, the *Fairy Queen*'s problems were just beginning. It turned out that the last wave to wash over the ship had almost put out the boiler fires. With little steam built up, the vessel was barely moving forward through the rough seas. The crew tried to use the jib sail, but could not get the steamer pointed into the wind enough for the sail to work properly.

When word reached the passengers that there was

trouble with the boilers, many left the cabin again to lend a hand. Some carried the wood stored on the forward deck down to the boilers, while others took any wooden furniture they could find to be used as firewood. This worked for a while, but the heavy seas had done more damage than anyone realized. Water continued to seep in under the boilers, and the fires were soon extinguished altogether. Consequently, the *Fairy Queen*'s engines ceased to work, and the ship was suddenly at the mercy of the sea.

Captain Belyea, who had remained at the wheel all this time, gave the order to lower the ship's anchor so that it would bring her into the wind, a position he hoped would keep her from taking on more water. The captain then gave over control of the ship to First Mate Patrick Treanor and went below to supervise the restarting of the boilers. He knew that without the engine, the steamer, as well as her passengers and crew, were in great peril.

Patrick Treanor was new to the *Fairy Queen*, replacing the regular mate, who was off visiting his sick wife. He had only been acting mate on the ship for about 12 days and perhaps wasn't as experienced as he should have been. As the vessel settled deeper in the water, broaching-to more frequently, one of the passengers, Edward Lydiard, suggested to Treanor that he run the boat aground at Pictou Island. Treanor rejected this idea, explaining that there was a small reef near the island that would tear the hull of the steamer to pieces before they even reached land.

Meanwhile, the sight that greeted Captain Belyea in the engine room was grim. The floor of the room was submerged, and the water level was rising quickly. Upon seeing this, the captain realized he would be unable to restart the boilers. He also recognized that the ship had to be leaking very badly to have that much water below the deck.

By this time, the weak October light had faded and nighttime had arrived. In the passenger cabin, Arabella and Alice De Wolfe sat as close together as possible. They tried to draw strength from each other and hoped they could hold up against the ordeal they knew might be ahead. As they observed the gentlemen passengers running to and fro between the cabin and upper deck, their anxiety grew. Soon there was the word from one of the men that open leaks were reported all over the ship and the engine room was flooding — the *Fairy Queen* wasn't only crippled, she was sinking. The sisters and their maid clung together for comfort while, nearby, the other female passengers prayed. The male passengers who were still in the cabin once again went to see if they could assist the captain.

Henry Pineo, who had taken shelter in the wheelhouse, watched as wave after wave broke over the ship's deck. When he saw some of his fellow passengers starting to bail, he left the wheelhouse to help them, but the water seemed to be coming in faster than they could get rid of it. Several of the passengers had to keep at the crew to continue bailing. At around 10 p.m., the captain called a halt to their efforts, saying there wasn't much hope in keeping the water out. For the 26 people on board the *Fairy Queen* that night, this was a pivotal moment. The order to stop bailing made everyone realize that their fight for survival — in a sea that would show them no mercy — was just beginning.

The ship's provisions were poor when it came to flotation devices. The *Fairy Queen* had no life buoys on board, but she did have two lifeboats — a large one capable of holding up to 24 people in calm water, and a smaller boat that could hold 8 to 10 people. For some reason, there were only four oars available between the two boats.

When First Mate Patrick Treanor saw there was no hope for the ship, he abandoned his post in the wheelhouse and readied the larger lifeboat for launching. As the first lifeboat was lowered into the stormy sea, Treanor and James Turner, the ship's clerk, climbed aboard, and the captain threw the mailbags in after them.

Upon seeing that the first of the lifeboats was being launched, several of the crew and one of the passengers, Hector McKinnon, jumped aboard as well. Angry at the sight, Henry Pineo turned to Captain Belyea and demanded to know why the lifeboat had been launched without first putting the women aboard. The captain explained that he wanted to get the first boat away from the ship because he was afraid it would be damaged from the violent waves beating against it. He then promised to get the women on the smaller boat, and he headed to the passenger cabin to speak to them.

The Fairy Queen

Arabella knew as soon as she saw the captain that he didn't have good news. He informed the women that they would soon be boarding a lifeboat and instructed them to dress warmly. He didn't confirm that the *Fairy Queen* was sinking, but the women all knew a call to the lifeboats meant it was no longer safe to stay on board the ship.

With resolution in their movements, the women began pulling on their shawls and scarves, preparing to face the autumn gale that was raging outside. They had all stayed below since coming on board and weren't sure what to expect when they went topside.

It was far worse than Arabella could have imagined. The *Fairy Queen*, which had seemed solid enough when she was tied to the wharf at Charlottetown, now appeared to be a tired old vessel that was barely floating. Her deck was riding so low in the water that almost every wave threatened to swamp her. Frightened at the sight, Arabella asked Captain Belyea how long it would be before they could leave the ship. The captain assured her that all the women would be loaded on to the smaller lifeboat as soon as it was lowered to the water.

This, however, turned out not to be the case. Instead, when the lifeboat hit the water, several crew members jumped aboard. Captain Belyea then told the passengers that he would lower himself down to the lifeboat to make sure that it stayed by the sinking vessel. He promised to hold it steady for the women to be put on board. Shocked, the passengers watched as the captain boarded the second lifeboat and a crew member let go of the rope holding both boats to the ship. Henry Pineo, standing aboard the sinking *Fairy Queen*, yelled to the captain to come back and get the women, but the men in the lifeboats did not raise an oar to try to get back to the ship. Slowly, the boats drifted away until the stranded passengers could barely see them.

Staring in astonishment at the disappearing lifeboats, Arabella realized there would be no rescue for her and Alice, or for the other passengers. All they could do now was attempt to retain their dignity on a vessel that would surely be their death. With little else but their shawls to protect them from raging storm, the women stood huddled together on the deck. Soon the spray from the waves had soaked through their clothing and, combined with the cold wind, chilled them to the bone. Suddenly, another huge wave swept over the ship and two passengers, Mr. Parker and Dr. MacKenzie, were swept overboard. Acting quickly, the other male passengers managed to get them a line and pull both men to safety.

Once he was back on board the doomed vessel, Dr. MacKenzie found a bottle and put a note in it telling of the passengers' abandonment by the captain and crew of the *Fairy Queen*. He also listed everyone's name so that, should they not make it through the storm, there would be some sort of record of what had happened and to whom.

A total of 17 people were left on board the sinking ship, and among them were a mere five crew members: Edmund and

Edward Inglis (cabin boys), Hugh O'Hara (the cook), Thomas Parker (the steward), and James Wadham (a deck hand).

For hours, the people on the *Fairy Queen* clung to the hope that the steamer would survive the tail end of the October storm. But the ship continued to settle lower and lower into the sea as the waters of the Northumberland Strait washed over her decks. A few of the passengers, including Henry Pineo and Mr. Parker, kept to the stern of the ship, while the others huddled together farther forward. All were wet, scared, and chilled to the bone, and all wondered how long they could hold on. At approximately 2 a.m. on October 8, the steamer, hit by one last devastating wave, broke apart and turned over.

By some miracle, part of the hurricane deck from the ship held together, and Henry Pineo and Mr. Parker climbed on board and held on tight. Soon, six others managed to swim through the waves to the makeshift raft.

At the same time, passenger Peter Cameron found himself on a smaller portion of the hurricane deck that had broken off from the larger raft. At one point, he raised his head and saw three women trying to reach a piece of wreckage, but the next time he looked up, they were gone. Moments later, he caught sight of fellow passenger Thomas McGuigan, who was struggling to swim to the larger raft. Suddenly, another wave came up and washed McGuigan away. Visibility got even worse, and Cameron soon lost sight of the larger part of the hurricane deck as he held on to his own piece of the deck for dear life.

For eight long hours, the violent seas tossed the large

raft about. The survivors clung to it in desperation, fearing they would capsize at any moment. Buffeted by the waves and pulled by the tides, the raft finally came ashore near New Glasgow, Nova Scotia. Half drowned, deeply chilled, and barely able to walk, the passengers stumbled off in search of help. Soon they were welcomed into nearby homes and given dry clothing and hot beverages. Their hosts listened in horror to the tale of the sinking of the *Fairy Queen*.

Although they were exhausted, three of the survivors — including Henry Pineo — insisted on making their way to the telegraph office in New Glasgow, where they sent a wire to Pictou alerting authorities to what had happened and demanding the arrest of the captain and crew who'd abandoned them.

Not surprisingly, the lifeboats carrying the deserters had both landed safely. The first and larger of the two had arrived at Carriboo, Nova Scotia, early in the morning of October 8, and the crew was taken in by local residents and given shelter and dry clothing. The smaller lifeboat, meanwhile, had made it to shore at Pictou around 3 a.m. Captain Belyea and the rest of the men on board the boat were also cared for by local residents.

Besides the crew in the two lifeboats, nine passengers had managed to make it ashore. Eight of these had been on the large makeshift raft, while the ninth, Peter Cameron, had held on to his own smaller raft until it finally landed near Big Harbour, Nova Scotia, hours after the other survivors had made it to safety.

The Fairy Queen

When word found its way back to the authorities in Pictou that another passenger had washed up on shore at Big Harbour, fishermen set out in their boats to search for more survivors. But there were none to be found. Instead, people searching the shoreline discovered pieces of wreckage from the steamer, as well as trunks belonging to Dr. MacKenzie and the DeWolfe sisters. Sadly, Arabella and Alice DeWolfe, and their maid, Jane, did not survive the ordeal. Nor did Dr. MacKenzie, whose decomposing body was found underneath a piece of the *Fairy Queen* that had washed ashore nearly a month after the tragedy.

When word of the sinking of the *Fairy Queen* began to circulate, people were extremely distressed. As they mourned the loss of life, they also questioned how it was that nearly the entire crew of the vessel was alive and well — only Thomas Parker, the steward, had died in the shipwreck. When it was discovered that most of the crew had abandoned the passengers, grief turned to anger, and the public wanted to see severe punishment for the captain and his crew, and justice for those who had drowned.

Captain Belyea and his crew were quickly arrested. Then, on October 28, 1853, there was a sitting of the Supreme Court of Nova Scotia at Pictou, where a grand jury indicted the captain and most of the crew for manslaughter. First Mate Patrick Treanor didn't help his cause any when he stated that he "would not have gone alongside the sinking ship again for five hundred pounds, not for all Pictou." The captain and crew were released on bail and ordered to appear at the Michaelmas session of the Supreme Court of Nova Scotia in Halifax.

Inquiries into the sinking of the *Fairy Queen* were held in Nova Scotia and Prince Edward Island. Fingers were pointed at the ship's owner, James Whitney, for the lack of safety equipment on board, and also for running a poorly kept ship. Whitney, it turned out, had a reputation for cutting corners. Although the *Fairy Queen* was only six years old, she had weathered some bad storms in the Northumberland Strait while delivering mail between Charlottetown, Pictou, and Shediac, New Brunswick. She had even run aground at Shediac a short time before her sinking. It was rumoured that in order to keep his contract as an official mail carrier for the provincial government of Prince Edward Island, Whitney had switched the engine of the *Fairy Queen* with one from an old wrecked steamer called the *North America*. The government of PEI was also severely censured for not inspecting the ship to make sure Whitney was abiding by all the rules and regulations set in place at the time.

As for the fate of Captain Belyea and his crew, the case against them was thrown out of court on a technicality. In the Easter Term, 1854, of the Supreme Court of Nova Scotia there appears a court summary of the findings of the Supreme Court Michaelmas session:

The Fairy Queen

The Queen v. William R. Belyea — April 7
The omission of the residences and occupations of
the grand jurors in the list, and in the panel, held
sufficient grounds for quashing an indictment for
felony.

Chapter 4
The *Marco Polo*

hroughout the 19th and early 20th century, New Brunswick was the centre of tall shipbuilding in Canada, producing over 50 percent of all tall ships in the country. Among these, the most famous was the *Marco Polo*, the fastest ship in the world.

The *Marco Polo* was built by James Smith, an Irishman who left his native country in 1820 with plans to live in Philadelphia. Somehow, he ended up in Saint John instead and found work as a carpenter in various shipyards before launching his first vessel, the *Ocean Queen*. Soon he had his own shipyard on the east side of Saint John Harbour in Courtney Bay, on the banks of a small inlet called Marsh Creek.

Smith's was not the only shipbuilding business in Marsh Creek. His main competition was a shipyard owned by

William and Richard Wright, who were reportedly building the biggest vessel ever to be constructed in Saint John. In 1850, they laid the 182-foot-long keel of the *Beejapore.*

Not to be outdone, Smith made plans of his own. He laid a 184-foot-long keel for his newest ship, a timber carrier that would haul deals of lumber across the Atlantic to Liverpool, England. The design for this ship combined the sleek underwater body of a clipper at the fore and aft, and the midship section of a cargo carrier. Named the *Marco Polo*, her frame was made with stout planks of tamarack, pitch pine, and oak.

On April 19, 1851, *The New Brunswick Courier* published a report of the ship's launching, which had occurred two days earlier:

> A large and elegant vessel called the *Marco Polo* was launched on Thursday morning last from the building yard of Mr. James Smith at Courtney Bay. He is also the owner. She has three complete decks, measures 1625 tons, and her length aloft is upwards of 184 feet. We presume that although not quite the largest that has been built in the Province this splendid ship is probably the longest that has been built in the Province. She is named after the celebrated Venetian traveller who discovered the coast of Malabar.

The launching of the *Marco Polo* had not been without incident. As the crowds had gathered along Marsh Creek to cheer her on, the crew had had problems holding the ship steady. She barreled down the launchway and into the water with such force that the launch ropes were ripped from the hands of the crew members. As a result, she plowed straight across the creek and into a mud bank on the other side.

Because of her size, the *Marco Polo* was stuck in the mud for two weeks before the high tides, combined with spring flooding, raised the water level enough in Marsh Creek for the ship to be hauled out. As it happened, those two weeks of lying slightly on her side in thick mud had caused some damage to the ship's keel — the middle was now six inches higher than the ends. Some mariners believe this permanent warp, or "hog" was the reason for her soon-to-be discovered speed. Others, however, credit her swiftness to the man who positioned her masts — John White, from Prince Edward Island. After the launching mishap, White's skill was sought out to place the masts in a position that would allow them to take advantage of the warp in the keel.

Whichever theory is true, the fact remains that the *Marco Polo* was fast. Her swiftness was evident even on her maiden voyage, which began on May 31, 1851. Under the command of Captain William Thomas of Saint John, she sailed from New Brunswick to Liverpool with a full cargo of timber in just 15 days. This was impressive, and soon the *Marco Polo* had a regular run. Under the command of

Captain Amos Crosby of Yarmouth, Nova Scotia, she carried cotton from Mobile, Alabama, to Liverpool. Her first round-trip voyage took only 30 days.

In 1852, while the *Marco Polo* was tied up at the dock in Liverpool, James Smith decided to sell his ship to Paddy McGee, a marine store dealer who often bought and sold ships and cargo from around the Liverpool port. Always one to keep up with the latest business trends, he knew there was an increase in trade and hoped to make a tidy profit by reselling the *Marco Polo* quickly.

As was the custom, McGee attached a broom handle to the mast of the ship to indicate she was for sale. In June 1852, she caught the eye of James Baines of the Black Ball Line, who was looking for ships to carry immigrants from England to Australia. There was a gold rush in Australia at the time, and more ships were needed as passenger carriers. And so, the *Marco Polo* was bought by the Black Ball Line and refitted for passenger use. Her hull was sheathed in copper, and cabins and compartments were constructed. The *Illustrated London News* published an article describing the refitting in February 1853:

> On deck forward of the poop which is used as a ladies cabin is a home on deck to be used as a dining saloon. It is ceiled with maple and the pilasters are panelled with richly ornamented and silvered glass, coins of various countries being a feature

of the decorations. The saloon doors are panelled in stained glass, bearing figures of commerce and industry from the designs of Mr. Frank Howard … The berths in separate state rooms are ranged in the 'tween decks and are rendered cheerful by circular glass hatchlights of novel and effective construction.

The refitting of the *Marco Polo* was everything James Baines had hoped it would be. On her first journey out as a passenger ship, she was under the command of James Nicol "Bully" Forbes, from Aberdeen, Scotland. Leaving Liverpool on July 4, 1852, the *Marco Polo* carried 930 passengers, 30 regular crew, and 30 people who worked in exchange for their passage. She sailed through Port Phillips Head and into Melbourne 76 days later on September 18, 1852 — a trip that took most ships anywhere from 100 to 120 days. Departing Melbourne on October 11, she took another 76 days to complete her return trip, arriving in Liverpool on December 26. In doing this, the *Marco Polo* became the first ship on record to journey from Liverpool to Melbourne and back in less than six months. As she sailed up the Mersey River, Captain Bully Forbes had his men fly a banner that read, "Fastest Ship in the World."

People were amazed at the *Marco Polo*'s speed and wondered if her first journey had been nothing more than a stroke of luck. But the fastest ship in the world lived up to her proud title. For the next 15 years, she carried immigrants to their destinations in record time, and her various captains and crews remained in awe of her remarkable swiftness and reliability. She was considered the unconquered Queen of the Seas.

As the *Marco Polo's* prowess became increasingly well known, her builder, James Smith, received numerous orders from companies who wanted a tall ship with her speed. Smith never did produce another ship with the swiftness and endurance of the *Marco Polo*, but her reputation alone brought the shipbuilders of New Brunswick world recognition as very skilled craftsmen — a spotlight which they thoroughly earned and enjoyed.

The life of the *Marco Polo* was riddled with heroic acts and misadventure. In August 1858, her captain and crew rescued the passengers and crew of the immigrant ship *Eastern City*, which had burned at sea near the Cape of Good Hope. Then, in 1861, the *Marco Polo* collided with an iceberg south of Cape Horn, badly damaging her hull. Soon after that, the Black Ball Line sold the ship, but her new owners still used her to carry immigrants from England to Australia. In fact, her last voyage to Australia in 1867 was made in the same time as her first voyage in 1852 — 76 days from Melbourne to Liverpool.

After 15 years of solid sailing, the *Marco Polo* was showing her age. In 1867, shortly after her return from Australia, she failed to pass the passenger survey. As a result, she was relegated from the prestigious passenger trade back to the general cargo trade. Her saloons and dining rooms were stripped of all their finery, and her passenger quarters were gutted to make way for cargo holds. Although she was suddenly forced into hauling coal, lumber, and cotton instead of transporting people, seamen worldwide still honoured her legend and saluted whenever they saw her.

In 1871, the famous ship was sold to Wilson & Blain Company from South Shields, England, and used to transport coal and timber. In 1874, her fine lines were further obscured when she was cut down and reduced to a barque rig. While waiting for a cargo of guano off the coast of Chile, she was severely damaged when her crew decided to land a 16-foot shark on board. The shark thrashed about the deck so much that it fell through the cabin skylight and had to be killed with an axe by the ship's carpenter. The cabin was more or less destroyed in the process.

Gradually, the *Marco Polo*'s beauty gave way to shabbiness. But she could still sail, and she still had some speed. In 1881, the ship changed hands again when she was sold to Bell & Lawes from South Shields. The next year, at the age of 31, she was sold to a Norwegian, Captain Bull of Christiania, who used her to haul lumber across the Atlantic between Europe and Canada.

In July 1883, the *Marco Polo* set sail from Montmorency, Quebec, with a cargo of pine deals for London. By then, her planking was water-soaked and warped, and her hull was held together with chains. Her water pumps worked day and night as water seeped in through her seams. Indeed, the once grand Queen of the Seas was dying.

Upon entering the Gulf of St. Lawrence, the *Marco Polo* was met by a wild summer gale. Both Captain Bull and his crew knew they were in trouble as the vessel was tossed about by the storm. Soon, wave after wave was crashing over the ship's deck. The crew had her pumps working double time, but couldn't keep up with the amount of water they were taking in through the leaks in her hull and the holes in her deck. The *Marco Polo* began riding lower in the sea.

Captain Bull quickly realized there was no way the ship would survive the storm. Her planks strained against the chains that were holding her together as the water level kept rising in the cargo hold. In desperation, the captain made the decision to try to beach the ship on the shoreline of Prince Edward Island. He ordered the crew to raise every piece of sail on the vessel.

The winds were blowing north-northeast at full hurricane force when Captain Bull aimed the bow of the *Marco Polo* toward the Cape Cavendish shore. With every sail straining in the storm, the grand old ship, riding very low in the water, held herself steady as she went aground on the rocks about 90 metres offshore. She continued to hold herself upright as the crew cut down her masts and rigging to prevent her drifting out to sea. Then, once the huge iron mainmast was cut down, and with it the mizzen-topmast, she broached-to.

Throughout the night, the grand old lady held herself together as waves crashed again and again against her aged hull. Meanwhile, the churning waters made it impossible for the crew to abandon the vessel, and they clung to the ship for dear life. Finally, morning arrived and the storm began to wane. With the help of some local fishermen, the captain and crew managed to get off the ship and make it to shore.

While the *Marco Polo* lay grounded, Captain Bull sold both the ship and her cargo to parties in Saint John, and a local company from the Cavendish area undertook the task of unloading the vessel. Armed with axes and saws, they cut away her upper deck in order to reach the cargo below. The once-revered vessel was soon reduced to a mere shell.

One evening, as the salvaging work continued, the men from the salvage company decided to stay on board the ship for the night. They were soon hit with another wild gulf storm. As the weather worsened, the men grew more and more certain that the ship would not be able to withstand another storm. Desperate to escape, three of the men left the ship and tried for shore only to have their boat swamped by the waves. Two of them managed to swim to safety, but the third drowned.

As those who had stayed behind on the *Marco Polo* held on to the old ship, a huge wave suddenly came crashing up her side, breaking and sinking the forecastle head. The only part of the ship left intact was a small portion of her bow, and the men clung to it firmly. Slowly, the storm abated, and by the next evening, a rescue party had brought the men safely to shore.

A week later, another storm washed away the remaining signs of the *Marco Polo* forever. Some say she had come home to Canada to die in familiar waters — only 240 kilometres from Marsh Creek, where she was first launched.

Today, the Queen of the Seas is not forgotten. Her proud history as the fastest ship in the world was a testament to her builder, James Smith, and to the captains and crew who sailed her. She is honoured by Canada through commemorative stamps, coins, historical novels, and documentaries.

Chapter 5
The *Union*

ack Dyre was looking for a change of pace. In 1889, jobs weren't plentiful in his hometown of Sussex, New Brunswick, and Dyre, who fancied himself an adventurous sort, wanted to find something new and exciting to do. He decided to look for work down the coast at St. Martins, which he knew to be a major shipbuilding centre.

Around the same time that Dyre was considering a change, a group of shipbuilders from St. Martins came up with the idea to build their own ship and use it in coastal trade with Nova Scotia and the United States. They would work as their own shipping agents, procuring contracts and delivering goods up and down the coast. These men, Captain John Kelly, Michael Kelly, George Cutten, John Burchill, and

Nathaniel MacCumber, pooled their resources and built a topmast schooner that they christened the *Union.*

Fortuitously, Jack Dyre landed in St. Martins right around the time that Captain John Kelly was recruiting crew members for the *Union,* and Dyre signed on as the ship's cook. The rest of the crew consisted of Frank McDonough, Edward Bradshaw, William Bradshaw, and Nelson Smith — all from St. Martins.

On April 10, 1889, the *Union* began her maiden voyage, sailing from Little Salmon River, near St. Martins, to Boston with a load of piling. The trip went smoothly, and the new crew members worked well together.

While they were still docked in Boston, Captain Kelly received a contract to pick up a load of deals from Shulee, Nova Scotia (across the Bay of Fundy from St. Martins), and to transport the cargo back to Boston. Soon after this trip, the *Union* landed several more contracts, and the captain and his crew were kept busy hauling cargo up and down the coast.

In August 1889, on one of their return trips to Shulee from Boston, Captain Kelly decided to make a stopover in St. Martins so that he and his crew could spend a night at home with their families. While his captain and crewmates eagerly headed to their respective homes, Dyre, having no family of his own in the immediate area, decided to stay on board the *Union.* He was pleased with his decision. The crew members were required to keep close quarters while working on the ship, and Dyre was looking forward to spending some time alone. He turned in around 10 p.m. and was fast asleep, gently rocked by the bobbing motion of the schooner.

Suddenly, a harsh, whispery voice roused him. "Dyre, leave this vessel," the voice said. At first he thought he was dreaming, but after a few moments he wasn't so sure. Pulling on some socks, he left his warm bed to check out the ship, just in case someone had come on board and was trying to scare him. Upon finding no one, he crawled back into his bunk and lit his pipe, hoping that a quiet smoke would calm his nerves.

Soon he was snuggled back under the covers, relaxed. He was nearly asleep when he heard the voice again: "Dyre, leave this vessel."

Dyre got up a second time and inspected every place he could think of where someone might hide. Once again, he found no one. Telling himself it was stupid to be so nervous, Dyre headed back to his bunk, had another smoke, and settled down for a sleep. It was well past midnight and he knew he needed to get some rest in order to perform his duties capably the next day. Just as he was dozing off, he heard the voice yet again: "Dyre, leave this vessel."

Now, mariners tend to be a superstitious bunch by nature, and even though Dyre had not spent much time on the water, he knew that hearing a strange voice telling him three times to leave a ship meant he should probably listen. This time when he got up, he got fully dressed, gathered his belongings, threw them out onto the breakwater, and then climbed up after them.

The next morning, Captain Kelly found Dyre on the breakwater, pale and trembling and pacing back and forth. The terrified cook told the captain that he wouldn't be able to make the voyage to Shulee, and that no amount of persuasion by Kelly would change his mind. Dyre also told the captain about the voice, but Kelly shrugged it off, insisting that the young man must have had a bad dream. Dyre remained unconvinced. He was certain something awful would happen to him if he went on the ship.

Seeing it would be impossible to get Dyre back on the schooner, Kelly realized he needed to find another cook for the voyage. He quickly spread word of his predicament around St. Martins, and another local man by the name of William Bradshaw offered to go. This meant there would be two William Bradshaws on board — a cook and an able seaman.

As soon as the second William Bradshaw was aboard, Captain Kelly gave the orders to raise the anchor. The *Union* left the breakwater and drifted up the Bay of Fundy toward Shulee. There was no breeze that morning, and the schooner was forced to move at the mercy of the tide. By noon, the tide was ebbing and the *Union* was drifting back down the bay. Then, at about 3 p.m., the tide turned again and the ship drifted up the bay once more.

As the hours passed, the schooner's big sails remained useless, and Captain Kelly could see that other vessels were having the same problem. At one point, the captain counted 40 other ships in the vicinity, all moving helplessly up and down the Bay of Fundy. The crews of these ships could do little but try to keep their vessels away from the shoreline as they drifted with the tide.

The lack of wind was putting the *Union* behind schedule, and Captain Kelly began to regret taking time for a stopover at St. Martins. The crew, meanwhile, was growing increasingly uneasy. They started to wonder if Dyre had been right to stay ashore — perhaps the trouble they were experiencing was, in fact, a sign of bad luck to come.

By late afternoon, dark clouds had gathered, but there was still no wind to catch the ship's sails. At this point, the *Union* was just off Fownes Head, about five kilometres east of St. Martins. Knowing that dark clouds meant rain was on its way, Captain Kelly decided to put on his foul weather gear, which was stored in the cabin, where crewman Nelson Smith was working. When Kelly entered the cabin, he told Smith of his intentions and suggested that Smith don his own gear.

Suddenly, there was a tremendous noise and the ship lurched to the side. A moment later, she flipped over completely, and Captain Kelly found himself standing on the ceiling of the cabin, with the floor over his head. He realized immediately that the *Union* had capsized, with full sails. Smith, who'd been standing closer to the doorway of the cabin, had dashed down the companionway to the deck when the ship started to turn over. Soon he was clinging to her overturned keel.

Captain Kelly could barely see in the dimness of the

cabin, but he managed to find the companionway and, taking a deep breath, dove down toward the deck. The captain knew he had little time to get out of the capsized vessel before the Bay of Fundy's frigid waters took their toll. With a great surge of power, he kicked his way free of the deck and came up on the side of the ship. He then managed to pull himself up onto the keel, joining the frightened Smith.

For the next 10 minutes or so, both men sat huddled on the keel of the *Union* while rain came down in torrents. Unable to spot the rest of the crew, they began to fear the worst. These fears were suddenly compounded by the strange sound of gunshots — the air that had been trapped below when the *Union* had overturned was now forcing its way out and, in the process, blowing some of the oakum out of the ship's seams.

When the sudden rain squall stopped, Kelly and Smith noticed that all the other ships in the bay were still floating upright — it appeared that only the *Union* had been affected by the storm. Upon seeing the two men on the hull of the ship, fishermen from St. Martins sent out a boat to rescue them. The other crew members, however, could not be found, and it was assumed they'd been swept overboard and drowned.

The following day, the tugboat *Lillie* arrived from Saint John to tow the *Union* back to the breakwater at St. Martins. Hundreds of people, including Jack Dyre, gathered to watch as the vessel was brought in.

Word of the *Union* capsizing had spread quickly throughout St. Martins, and people were shocked by what had happened. As they waited for the tugboat to appear with the ship, they all wondered how exactly the disaster could have occurred, especially given the fact that there had been no strong winds when the ship had capsized, only heavy rains. Moreover, usually when a sailing vessel overturned with her sails set, the sails held the ship on her side for a while before she completely capsized. But this hadn't happened with the *Union* — a fact that confounded the sea captains and shipbuilders of the community. What strange force of nature had caused the schooner to flip over with full sails?

As the *Lillie* neared the breakwater with the upsidedown *Union* in tow, the mast of the *Union* started to snag on the sand, causing enough of a motion for the schooner to right herself with her sails still intact. The crowd that had gathered could only stare in amazement as the ship slowly rolled upright. How could it be that the *Union* suffered no damage to her sails? The people of St. Martins were mystified.

As soon as the ship was safely in the harbour, Captain Kelly arranged to have someone pump the excess water from her hold and cabin area in order to assess if any damage had been done. In the process of pumping the water, however, workers discovered the body of William Bradshaw — the man who had replaced Jack Dyre as cook. Bradshaw's body was found in the galley, where he'd gone to start preparations for the evening meal just before the vessel had capsized. When Jack Dyre heard this bit of news, he was once again thankful he'd listened to that strange voice telling him to get off the ship.

The bodies of the *Union*'s remaining crew members — Frank McDonough, Edward Bradshaw, and able seaman William Bradshaw — were never recovered. This made the disaster all the more difficult for their loved ones. Meanwhile, the businessmen who owned shares in the *Union* were also affected by the tragedy, but they felt that life — and work — had to go on. The *Union* was soon repaired and back in service.

A few years later, on August 18, 1892, she was sold to a company called Shields and Vaughan from the Point Wolfe area in Albert County, east of St. Martins. For the next several years she carried lumber from sawmills in that area to New England.

In the fall of 1917, the *Union* was on her way to St. Andrews, New Brunswick, with a load of fertilizer from Boston when she encountered a terrible storm off the coast of Maine. As violent winds assaulted the schooner, her rigging came crashing down, wrenching apart the deck boards and allowing the sea to flow in. The aging ship could not withstand the pressure of the water. Soon, many of her seams were giving way and she was riding very low in the water. With her mast and rigging gone, the crew knew they would not be able to sail the schooner to safety. They had no choice but to abandon ship in their lifeboat and head for the Maine coast.

The *Union* remained abandoned at sea for several weeks and quickly became a serious navigational hazard to other ships in the area. On October 26, 1917, a French man-of-war ship patrolling the coast sank the derelict schooner and sent her to the bottom of the Atlantic.

No one ever came up with a definite explanation for what happened to the *Union* when she capsized on that fateful day in August 1889. Experts offered many theories, suggesting that everything from a violent cross wind to a sudden lightning strike were responsible for the tragedy. Others continued to believe that a supernatural force of some kind had caused the disaster. Whatever the case, one thing was certain: to his dying day, Jack Dyre remained grateful that he'd followed the mysterious order to "Leave this vessel."

Chapter 6
The *Royal Tar*

Imagine it: a crisp fall day with a hint of frost in the air. The leaves are changing colour, people are bustling about, and horses are hauling carts laden with goods up and down the streets. These were all typical sights in Saint John, New Brunswick, in October 1836. Not so typical, however, was the cargo on a group of wagons that were slowly making their way toward the harbour. The wagons were carrying cages filled with exotic animals.

It was October 21, and Fuller's Menagerie, which had been touring Nova Scotia and New Brunswick for the last six months, was leaving Saint John and heading back to the United States. Young and old people alike stood and watched with wonder as the colourfully painted wagons, some large and some small, slowly descended King Street in the heart of the city to the wharf and loading docks below.

Fuller's Menagerie was like most other travelling circuses of the day: a mix of close-knit families and performers who had been together for a long time. It had the usual circus animals, including two camels, an elephant, a lion, a couple of tigers, ponies, and horses that were used both for performing and for pulling the wagons. It also had an impressive assortment of captive birds and reptiles.

With an entire circus to transport back to the United States, the owners of Fuller's Menagerie needed a large, reliable ship. They chose the *Royal Tar*, a 400-ton, 160-foot side-paddle steamer that could accommodate all of their animals and bring them to the U.S. in a relatively short period of time. The circus owners were anxious to get to New York, where they were hoping to find work for the winter.

Built in 1835 in Carleton, New Brunswick, the *Royal Tar* was more reliable than other ships because she had both a paddle wheel and sails. Her master, Thomas Reed, was a popular and efficient captain who believed in running a tight ship and a professional crew.

The *Royal Tar* had a regular route, which ran between Digby, Nova Scotia, Saint John, and Portland, Maine. This route enabled people to reach New York from Saint John in less than four days. With favourable winds and tide, the *Royal Tar* could make the journey from Saint John down the Bay of Fundy to Portland (with a stop in Eastport) in one day.

The Royal Tar

Once in Portland, passengers then had the choice of overland travel or transferring to another ship for sailing on to Boston and New York.

The passenger list for this October 21 sailing was longer than the usual 30 to 50 names. Joining the animals and employees of Fuller's Menagerie were a number of Irish immigrants, most of who were travelling in the steerage section and heading to the U.S. in hope of finding work. There were also several passengers travelling in the ship's cabin section. In all, 93 people (including crew) were on board the *Royal Tar* for the trip.

There was only a slight breeze blowing when, at 11 a.m., the *Royal Tar* slowly made her way out of Saint John Harbour and into the Bay of Fundy. As the ship sailed away, the circus band played "God Save the King" and Mogul the elephant trumpeted loudly at the noise.

Shortly after the steamer started her journey, the weather began to deteriorate, with gusty autumn winds driving straight up the Bay of Fundy. The first port of call was Eastport, and the *Royal Tar* had little problem arriving on schedule. However, when the ship left Eastport that evening, Captain Reed decided the conditions were too rough to continue on to Portland. He gave orders to the crew to manoeuvre the ship into Little River, near Cutter, Maine, in order to seek shelter from the storm.

As the winds battered the vessel, Captain Reed decided to keep the ship in the shelter of Little River for the weekend.

An experienced captain, he knew that the rough seas would damage the paddles on the steamer if he were to venture back into the open water.

For the passengers aboard the *Royal Tar*, the short voyage to Portland from Saint John was taking a lot longer than they'd anticipated. Parents were left with little to do but try to keep their children amused. Of course, the circus animals on board must have provided the youngsters with a great deal of entertainment. The children were likely delighted at the sight of the monkeys, zebra, and snakes that were kept under lock and key. And they must have been thrilled to hear the lion and tigers roar, the parrots talk, and the elephant trumpet. Too large to be stored anywhere else, Mogul was kept on deck with his handler close by.

By Monday, October 24, Captain Reed decided the seas were calm enough to continue on with the trip, so the *Royal Tar* left the safety of Little River. But, soon after the ship's departure, the heavy seas and strong westerly winds forced the captain to seek out shelter again — this time in Machias Bay. The wind finally changed direction the next day, becoming easterly, and Captain Reed once again started out for Portland.

During this time, however, the ship's second engineer failed to notice that the water levels in the boilers, which provided steam to the paddle wheel, were running very low. When the main engineer came on duty at 1 p.m., he saw the low levels and quickly informed Captain Reed that they had to get fresh water right away or else the boilers would likely explode. The captain immediately stopped the engines, and the safety valves were opened. The *Royal Tar* was about three kilometres from the Fox Islands in Penobscot Bay when her anchor was dropped.

In order to get the steam to the correct pressure for running the paddle wheel, the fires had to be completely extinguished in the furnaces, the boilers had to be refilled, and then the fires had to be restarted. Captain Reed personally supervised the extinguishing of the fires in the furnaces. Then, just as the crew started to fill the boilers with water, the steward, William Brown, noticed smoke rising around a portion of the deck directly above the boilers. He ran to tell the captain that the *Royal Tar* was on fire.

Without the paddle wheel working, Captain Reed knew he'd have to use the ship's sails and run the *Royal Tar* ashore in order to get the passengers to safety as soon as possible. In the meantime, he ordered the crew to use the pump they were filling the boilers with to fight the fire. However, dense smoke and flames soon made it impossible for the crew to man the water pumps.

At this point, Captain Reed gave the order to man the boats, and people rushed toward the lifeboats. Unfortunately, the engineer, other members of the crew, and several passengers had already secretly lowered the largest lifeboat and were pulling toward Isle au Haut, some 14 kilometres away, instead of heading directly for shore to get help.

As the flames ate at the decking, the abandoned passengers started to move toward the one remaining lifeboat. Realizing they would capsize if everyone piled in at once, Captain Reed rushed ahead, pushed off in the small boat, and then ordered the passengers to jump over the side of the burning steamer. Once passengers landed in the water, Captain Reed brought them alongside of the lifeboat with the use of his oar and then helped them climb aboard. Soon the boat was full and the captain moved to a safe position a short distance from the ship.

The *Royal Tar* presented an awful spectacle to those sitting helpless in the lifeboat. The fire was consuming the middle of the ship and the passengers and crew left on board were being driven to either end by the intensity of the heat and flames. Mogul, who had somehow gotten loose in the ruckus, was trumpeting loudly. The sounds of passengers screaming and animals screeching sent cold shivers down the spines of those huddled in the lone lifeboat.

By this time, the fire on the *Royal Tar* could be seen as far away as Belfast and Castine, Maine. Soon, the U.S. revenue cutter *Veto* from Castine appeared on the scene. Captain Reed boarded the newly arrived ship and explained the situation. Then, borrowing a small craft, he and William Brown (the *Royal Tar*'s steward), along with two seamen from the *Veto*, made numerous trips to the burning steamer in the small lifeboats, picking up as many passengers as possible and delivering them to the safety of the cutter.

Each trip was very dangerous. Most of the passengers were hysterical, and the captain worried that they would try to rush the small boat and swamp it. Some of the women, with their children in arms and their clothing afire, threw themselves forcefully from the burning vessel in order to douse the flames.

Meanwhile, many of the circus animals were dying from smoke inhalation, and many more were burned to death in their cages. The camels and horses were backed off the ship by their handlers, who hoped they would somehow swim to shore. And other animals jumped from the burning steamer of their own volition, without bothering anyone.

Mogul, however, was a difficult animal. He ran up and down the deck, trumpeting wildly as the flames continued to engulf the ship. Feeling the scorching heat against his skin, the terrified elephant finally jumped, aiming straight for a makeshift raft that was floating on the waves below. With a mighty crash he hit the raft, causing it to break apart and throwing its occupants into the churning water. Several people drowned, while others managed to cling to pieces of the broken raft. Mogul, in the meantime, finally got his bearings and began to swim toward the shoreline.

For almost four hours, Captain Reed and William Brown worked to rescue the remaining passengers on the burning steamer. When they were satisfied that they'd picked up all the survivors, the captain and his steward boarded the U.S. revenue cutter.

Overloaded with people, the *Veto*, altered her course for Isle au Haut. Fighting against the winds, the cutter finally managed to reach the safety of the island at around 7 p.m. Soon after landing on shore, the rattled survivors of the *Royal Tar* were met with a maddening surprise: the 16 men who had taken off in the largest lifeboat were all there, sitting comfortably around the fire at Squire Kimballs, one of the local lodgings. The other passengers were shocked to see these men enjoying themselves as if nothing had happened.

Despite their ire, the survivors managed to show their gratefulness to the people of Isle au Haut, who graciously provided them with warm clothing, food, and lodging. Hours after they'd settled in for the night, the burning *Royal Tar* remained visible in the distance as she drifted out to sea.

Later, Captain Reed and William Brown returned to Saint John aboard the schooner *Ploughboy* to a hero's welcome. Their efforts in rescuing the passengers of the *Royal Tar* were widely lauded, and the people of Saint John celebrated their bravery.

Sadly, the captain's triumphant return was quickly quelled by more bad news. While he was gone, his seven-year-old son had taken ill very suddenly and had died within two days. Captain Reed had arrived home just in time for his son's funeral.

This tragedy, however, did not stop the outpouring of gratitude. As the days passed, numerous letters praising both

Captain Reed and William Brown were published in the local newspapers. There were also many letters to the editors of various newspapers throughout Maine and New Brunswick decrying the actions of the 16 men who had abandoned their fellow travellers. A sarcastic newsman, who ridiculed these men publicly for their "callous feelings toward humanity," dubbed them the Humane 16.

In response, some of these same 16 men wrote letters to various newspapers in an attempt to justify their actions, describing their own misfortunes in the tragedy. The public, however, did not buy these justifications. Instead, many letter writers insisted the group be punished for their deeds, while many others wished them ill health and poor fortune.

As the Humane 16 were strongly criticized, Captain Reed and his steward continued to earn accolades. In acknowledgment of his bravery, the captain was presented with a cheque from the mayor and businessmen of Saint John. Meanwhile, the young men of the city presented William Brown with a medal and a small sum of money. One side of the medal was inscribed "*Royal Tar* October 25, 1836," and showed a representation of the burning steamer with her boats and the *Veto* coming to the rescue of the passengers. On the reverse side, an inscription read: "*The Inhabitants of Saint John, NB to W.G. Brown — As thine hand was to many, be some guardian hand to thee throughout every danger.*"

A man of honour, Captain Reed was generous in his

praise of the help he received from others during the tragedy. Below is a letter written by the captain and published in the *Weekly Chronicle* on November 4, 1836:

> Thomas Reed, Master of the late steamer *Royal Tar*, begs to tender his sincere thanks to Captain Howland Dyer, commanding the United States Cutter *Veto*, and his crew, for their great exertions in saving the survivors from the steamer when on fire in Penobscot Bay, on the 25th October: and also to Capt. William Barter, Captain George Kimbal, Capt. William Yeaton, Mr. Nathan Sawyer, Mr. Samuel Turner, Mr. Eben Sawyer, and Mr. Wm. Staples, all inhabitants of the Isle of Haut, for their humane attention to the sufferers. – St. John, 29th Oct. 1836.

The total loss of life that day was devastating. Out of the 93 people on board the *Royal Tar*, 32 perished, including 10 children from the steerage section and 3 crew members. The vessel and her cargo were worth around $200,000, but nothing was insured. The strongbox from Fuller's Menagerie, with all of its earnings from an entire summer of hard work, was lost — as were all the troupe's possessions.

The elephant, Mogul, managed to make it to shore, and two of the horses from the circus were later found wandering in a farmer's field. But there was no sign of the camels or other exotic animals. Moreover, four members of the troupe were also lost in the wreck.

The Irish immigrants who were travelling on the steamer lost not only any money they had on board, but also all of their clothing and anything else of value they were travelling with. Strangers in a strange land, they were left with only the clothes on their backs.

Chapter 7
The SS *Caribou*

While Atlantic Canadians have known many marine tragedies whose causes can be linked to fierce storms, man's inability to conquer the elements, or just poor judgment on the part of a captain or crew, they have also known tragedies of another sort — deliberate tragedies, caused by a cool, calculating enemy. Among the most heartbreaking of these was the sinking of the SS *Caribou*.

It was 1942, and the world was at war. While loved ones were off fighting overseas, daily life in Atlantic Canada went on as usual. Still, the signs of warfare were present everywhere on the East Coast. Military personnel could be spotted on practically every street of every city. Fathers, sons, and friends were regularly signing up to join the military, and almost every citizen knew an enlisted person. Newfoundland in particular bustled with activity. Home to several important military bases, the large, isolated rock served as a "jumping off" place for men and women from all branches of the Canadian military, as well as American and British personnel.

At that time, travelling to Newfoundland from mainland Canada meant having to take a ferry. The SS *Caribou* was the link between Port aux Basques, Newfoundland, and North Sydney, Nova Scotia. Built in Rotterdam, Holland, in 1925, the *Caribou* was first brought to St. John's for service on the Gulf of St. Lawrence. Made of steel, she could accommodate 150 first-class passengers and 250 second-class passengers, and had the capacity to hold about 1100 tons of cargo. This made her an ideal vessel for carrying passengers and cargo over the Cabot Strait, the 160 kilometres of water that lay between North Sydney and Port aux Basques. Soon, she became a ferry vessel for the Newfoundland Railway.

On the afternoon of Tuesday, October 13, 1942, the scene at the North Sydney ferry terminal was that of organized chaos as the *Caribou* was readied for her 8 p.m. departure. The shouts of the men working the port could be heard as they loaded the vessel's hold with cargo, which included 50 head of cattle, hundreds of bags of mail, and goods bound for the shelves of local merchants and military bases.

Meanwhile, passengers were making their way to the terminal, eager to board the ship. Among them was Gladys

Shiers, who had travelled by train from Halifax with her 15-month-old son, Leonard, to catch the ferry to Newfoundland. In their haste to make the train, Gladys had forgotten one of Leonard's favourite toys, and he'd cried for the plaything for most of the ride. Gladys, only 20 years old, was also three months pregnant with her second child, and her nerves were stretched to the limit. She and her husband, Elmer, were making their new home in St. John's, where he was stationed as a naval petty officer.

By late afternoon, people were lining up to board the ferry. There were 191 tickets purchased for the crossing — the *Caribou* would be carrying 118 military personnel, 73 civilians, and 46 crew on this particular trip.

Once their tickets were examined, the passengers were assigned accommodations and shown to their cabins by the ship's stewards. The women were given berths in the upper-deck cabins, while the men were accommodated in the cabins between decks. As the stewards escorted the *Caribou* passengers to their lodgings, they handed out life belts and pointed out the locations of the lifeboat stations and life jackets.

The *Caribou* had just finished a lengthy refit that, among other things, had provided improvements to her lifesaving equipment. The ship carried 14 carley floats, or rafts, which were bolted down to the decks, and six new lifeboats, one of which had a radio apparatus on board. The lifeboats were divided up so there were three on each side of the *Caribou*: two located amidships and one near the stern of the vessel. The captain of the ship, Ben Taverner, had also taken the extra precaution of making sure all four amidships lifeboats were swung out of their davits so they were ready for quick use. Though he saw no need to carry out a lifeboat drill, Captain Taverner had given his crew strict orders to show each of the passengers which lifeboat station they were to report to in case of an emergency.

There was good reason for the extra precautions. A month earlier, the armed yacht HMCS *Racoon* and the corvette HMCS *Charlottetown* had been torpedoed in the St. Lawrence River — proof that the Germans had been able to penetrate Canada's meagre coastline defenses.

The most recent sinking, and the one that really worried Captain Taverner, was that of the SS *Waterton* on the Cabot Strait just three days earlier. The *Waterton*, a 2410-ton British freighter, had been travelling from Corner Brook, Newfoundland, to Sydney with a load of paper when she was torpedoed in broad daylight. After hearing news of the *Waterton*'s demise, Captain Taverner and his crew knew it was only a matter of time before they, too, were attacked. With regular scheduled sailings between North Sydney and Port aux Basques, the *Caribou* was an easy target.

The sinking of the *Waterton* also proved there were U-boats actively working the local waters. Captain Taverner had orders to run under "blackout" conditions and to sail in a zigzag pattern to be less of a target. In addition, wartime regulations stipulated that all ships sailing in these waters required an escort. For this particular journey, the *Caribou* would be under the escort of the Royal Canadian minesweeper HMCS *Grandmere*.

Before the war, the *Caribou* had always travelled during the day, but now the ferry was required by the navy to make the crossing at night. Captain Taverner argued over this change with his superiors at Newfoundland Railway on more than one occasion. An experienced seaman, he believed it would be easier to carry out surveillance of the journey in the light of day, as both the navy ships and anti-submarine planes had a better chance of spotting enemy craft in daylight. Moreover, should something happen, the survival of the *Caribou*'s passengers and crew seemed more likely if the ship were to sink during the day. Taverner was unsuccessful in his arguments, however, and so he prepared for another night crossing with a navy escort.

When the *Caribou*'s whistle sounded the warning that she would soon be departing, there was a scurry of activity as last minute checks were carried out and people said goodbye to friends and family. At 8 p.m., just as the ship's gangways were being pulled up, Bob Newman, a merchant from Newfoundland, came running at full speed toward them. Leaping into the air, he landed safely on the deck as the crew laughed and shook their heads. Newman, a regular passenger on the *Caribou*, was frequently late for the ferry. Purser Tom Fleming added another name to the passenger list and the

SS *Caribou*, with 192 passengers and 46 crew, set sail for Port aux Basques.

Meanwhile, HMCS *Grandmere* was docked at the naval yards in Sydney, a short distance from North Sydney. Her crew of nearly 100, under the command of Lieutenant James Cuthbert, was preparing the ship for her trip as escort to the *Caribou*. The *Grandmere* was a Bangor class minesweeper with a top speed of 15 knots. Though she was equipped with an underwater detection device called an asdic, which was good for long-range detection, the vessel did not have radar that could be used to scan for vessels on the surface. Lieutenant Cuthbert, a Scottish-born career navy man, knew that the *Grandmere* was not an ideal escort, but felt she was better protection than some of the other escort vessels that had accompanied ships in the area.

The *Grandmere* had orders to follow the *Caribou* at a distance of approximately a quarter mile. These orders, set out in the "Western Approach Convey Instructions," did not sit well with the lieutenant. He believed his ship would be much more useful if she were to sail in front of the escorted vessel. This way, the asdic could detect the engine sounds of any approaching U-boats. Tucked in behind as she was ordered to be, all the minesweeper would be able to detect were the sounds of the *Caribou's* engines, leaving the crew of the *Grandmere* deaf to approaching submarines. Though Cuthbert had argued this point with his superiors, his arguments had fallen on deaf ears. And so, the *Grandmere* headed out of port to the rendezvous point, where she fell in behind the *Caribou* and began her escort duties across the Cabot Strait.

The increase of enemy activity in Atlantic coastal waters at the time had come from orders issued by Grand Admiral Karl Donitz of the German U-boat command. Under these orders, German submarine commanders were to target warships, freighters, and other vessels in an effort to prevent North American reinforcements from reaching Britain. The German naval commanders hoped that by keeping the Allied forces focussed on their own coastal waters, the Nazis would have a chance to reign supreme in the North Atlantic and defeat the British forces. However, the increase in U-boat activity along the Atlantic coastline had also resulted in increased surveillance during the day by the Royal Canadian Air Force's anti-submarine aircraft.

On the night of October 13, as the *Caribou* and *Grandmere* were making their way to Port aux Basques, Lieutenant Ulrich Graf of German submarine U-69 was bringing his vessel up from the depths of the Cabot Strait to air it out and recharge its batteries. With the increased patrols in the area during the day, it was necessary for the submarine to stay submerged until late at night, when there was less chance of being noticed. U-69 had been navigating the Atlantic coastal waters for nearly two months and had managed to get within 280 kilometres of Quebec City, where it had attacked a convoy of seven ships and sunk the freighter *Carolus* before slipping back out to the Atlantic to hunt again.

When U-69 surfaced for air that night, it was within 30 kilometres of Port aux Basques and just south of the route the *Caribou* was taking. Captain Taverner, aboard the *Caribou*, was sailing a zigzag course, as per his orders, and looking forward to arriving at Port aux Basques in a few hours. The journey from North Sydney to Port aux Basques usually took the ferry 8 to 10 hours, depending on the roughness of the seas. Although the waters were often rough in October, the ocean had only a medium swell on this trip.

All was quiet aboard the *Caribou* in the early morning hours of October 14. Most of her passengers had long bedded down for the night, and the majority of the crew who were not on duty had gone to bed, too. However, there were several people on board who were too restless to sleep, and some of them sat in the main lounge, smoking, playing cards, and talking quietly.

Captain Taverner was among those who could not sleep. He usually took the opportunity in the early morning to get a little rest, but for some reason, he couldn't settle down this time. At 1:50 a.m., the captain joined the purser, Tom Fleming, in the wireless room. Taverner mentioned to Fleming that he didn't like the alternate route they were sailing and was worried that the smoke coming from the *Caribou* could be easily seen on such a clear night.

At around 3:20 a.m., U-69 was cruising along on the surface of the water when Lieutenant Graf noticed two ships and identified them in the log as a freighter-passenger vessel with a small escort, possibly a destroyer, following behind. Quickly, the lieutenant ordered a change of course so that the U-boat was slightly ahead of the lead vessel and in a better position to torpedo the ship's starboard side.

Graf had positioned his submarine well, and, as the two vessels came within range, his crew aimed and fired. At approximately 3:30 on the morning of October 14, a torpedo from U-69 struck the *Caribou* on her starboard side amidships. The ensuing explosion shook the whole ship, causing some of the slumbering passengers to fall out of their beds as furniture and hand luggage flew about. Most of the crew in the ferry's engine room, and an unknown number of passengers and crew who had accommodations on the starboard side of the ship, were killed outright. Others were trapped inside compartments that had buckled from the blast and were unable to get topside. The torpedo also destroyed the two lifeboats located amidships on the starboard side, as well as the radio installation, so radioing for help was out of the question.

There was panic and confusion among the surviving passengers and crew. Some were dazed from being woken from sleep, while others wondered if the ferry had crashed into the wharf at Port aux Basques. But there were many on board, including the military personnel, who realized immediately what had happened.

It soon became evident to everyone that the ship was in trouble. Mothers grabbed their children and courageously pushed their way through the darkened corridors of the crippled ship. The military personnel on board pulled on whatever clothes they could find and tried to help the civilian passengers topside and toward the lifeboats.

Suddenly, a second series of explosions rocked the *Caribou*. As the boilers in her engine room exploded, she started to take on water at an alarming rate. Passengers streamed onto the deck and headed for the lifeboats positioned amidships on the port side. There was a problem, though: the seacocks (the valves used to release water that has gathered in the bottom of a boat) on both lifeboats had been left open, and when the boats were lowered they quickly began to take on water. Crew on one of the lifeboats managed to seal its valve, but the other boat was so crowded with people that it capsized before the seacock could be closed. Though passengers were able to right the boat, it capsized three more times. Finally, the people aboard gave up and, instead of trying to roll it back over, hung on to its overturned hull.

The two lifeboats at the stern of the ship were never launched. Terrified passengers, unfamiliar with the launching process, had climbed aboard while the boats were still fixed in their davits. No amount of persuasion by the crew could get the people aboard the lifeboats to climb out, and, as a result, the boats could not be released.

In all the chaos, Gladys Shiers, carrying baby Leonard, managed to find her way up from her cabin only to discover that the deck was already covered with water. Though she had trouble seeing anything because of the enforced blackout, she finally found a set of stairs leading to the bridge of the ship — the only area not covered by water. As she tried her best to soothe Leonard, the *Caribou* started to shake. Another explosion hit, tearing the child from her arms and throwing him overboard. Seconds later, Gladys herself was hurled overboard by another blast.

As a series of explosions continued to rock the *Caribou*, Tom Fleming and Captain Taverner tried to release more of the carly rafts, but a foot of water was covering the deck and they couldn't get the damaged levers to release. Straightening up, Captain Taverner left the rafts and walked toward the bridge. Jack O'Brien, a surviving crew member, later stated that the last thing he saw before jumping overboard was Ben Taverner standing on the bridge, ready to go down with his ship.

Within five minutes of the torpedo hitting the vessel, the *Caribou* had begun her long slide below the water's surface to settle on the bottom of the Cabot Strait. Panic reigned as passengers and crew still on board the sinking vessel jumped overboard. The water around the ferry was soon teeming with people desperately hanging on to floats and other pieces of debris. All around, passengers were screaming in the darkness. The lifeboats filled with water as people tried to climb on board. Others, weakened by their injuries or in shock from the frigid water, were too tired to attempt to swim to any of the boats and slowly drifted away.

The SS Caribou

Gladys Shiers was knocked unconscious by the explosion and came to in the cold waters of the Cabot Strait. By some miracle there was a life raft close by, and she climbed aboard. However, the raft brought little relief; there was no sign of baby Leonard, and Gladys had lost hope of finding him. Not only had she lost her son, she also feared that the shock of being in the cold water had harmed her unborn child.

As it turned out, Leonard was safe on another raft. Petty Officer Ralph Rogers had been flung from the ship by the same blast that had sent the child flying from Gladys's arms. Just as Leonard had come back to the surface of the water, so had Rogers. Grabbing the child, the petty officer made his way through the debris to a raft that was barely distinguishable in the dark. Upon recognizing the form of the child, people on the raft immediately made room for the pair, and soon Leonard was being passed from person to person as everyone on board took turns trying to keep him warm.

As the *Caribou* sank, the crew of the *Grandmere* reeled in shock. The initial explosion on the ferry, which had illuminated the black night, was the first indication to Lieutenant Cuthbert and his men that an enemy vessel was in the vicinity. The flash of the explosion had revealed the German submarine sitting defiantly on the water's surface. Spotting the U-boat, the *Grandmere*'s crew rushed into action. As one crew member sent word by radio that the *Caribou* had been hit by a torpedo, the minesweeper headed at full speed toward the submarine.

Lieutenant Graf of U-69, realizing the intent of what he considered to be a destroyer class vessel, and one that could overtake the submarine if it stayed on the surface, had only one option: he gave the order to dive. The U-boat circled around and took shelter some 450 feet beneath the surface of the water, close to where the *Caribou* had been hit. By doing this, Graf was certain the sub would be safe; there was no way the destroyer would dare throw depth charges near the *Caribou* survivors in the water.

The *Grandmere* did, in fact, drop depth charges, but in the location where the crew had last seen the submarine dive. When there was no explosion, Lieutenant Cuthbert knew the U-boat had probably managed to escape.

As the *Grandmere* neared the many survivors kicking and thrashing about in the waves, the crew of the minesweeper was torn over what to do next. Cuthbert's naval orders, however, were clear — hunting down the submarine was his top priority, even if it meant leaving survivors in the water. Bypassing the survivors was one of the hardest things Lieutenant Cuthbert would have to do in his naval career.

After several hours of fruitless searching, Cuthbert gave up looking for the submarine and issued the order to head back toward the position of the sinking vessel in the hope of picking up survivors. It was 5:20 a.m. and the eastern sky was just starting to lighten. At first, the crew of the *Grandmere* could find no one as the minesweeper navigated slowly through the water, but by 6:30 a.m., they were picking up a few survivors.

Meanwhile, word had made it to Port aux Basques that the *Caribou* was in trouble. The Newfoundland Railway agent, a Mr. George, chartered as many schooners and fishing vessels as possible to head out and assist in rescue operations. News of the disaster quickly spread throughout the town, and local buildings were made into temporary hospitals as the people of Port aux Basques waited for the rescue vessels to return with victims.

By 7:30 a.m., the crew of the *Grandmere* found themselves in the middle of a strange collection of lifeboats, hatches, rafts, and ship debris — all of which desperate passengers were clinging to. Also among the floating objects were many lifeless bodies bobbing up and down in the ocean swell. Overhead, an air force amphibious airplane was flying low in an attempt to locate more survivors, and also keeping watch in case of another submarine attack.

As the morning brightened, the winds started to pick up, making the sea choppy. It became increasingly difficult to get the survivors aboard the *Grandmere*. Many were too weak and numbed by the cold to help themselves, and several members of the *Grandmere*'s crew had to jump into the water to assist them. Using a scrabble net that was quickly thrown over the side of the ship, the crew pushed, pulled, and cajoled the survivors into climbing aboard.

Among those pulled onto the minesweeper was Gladys Shiers. The long night had taken its toll on the young mother, and as she got on board the *Grandmere* she slipped back into unconsciousness. Meanwhile, Petty Officer Ralph Rogers carried her son Leonard on board, but then collapsed from the cold soon afterward.

By 9:30 a.m., Lieutenant Cuthbert's vessel was carrying as many survivors as he could find, and his men were reaching the point of exhaustion from their efforts to bring them aboard. More rescue vessels were arriving at the site and would continue the search, so Cuthbert, following orders from his superiors, prepared to head back to the *Grandmere*'s home base of Sydney. (Even though Port aux Basques was closer, Cuthbert's superiors felt the survivors would be better off in Sydney, which had a modern naval hospital.)

In all, the *Grandmere* was able to rescue 104 people. Two of the survivors pulled from the cold autumn waters, however, died before the *Grandmere* left the search area — a young naval man by the name of William Glasgow and an unknown, blond, blue-eyed baby boy. This left a total of 102 survivors. Of the 237 people originally on board the *Caribou*, 11 navy personnel, 16 other military personnel, and 60 civilians survived. Of the crew of 46, 15 survived, including just one officer — the purser, Tom Fleming.

The only child to survive the wreck was Leonard Shiers. He and his pregnant mother were reunited for a brief moment aboard the *Grandmere* before Leonard was taken away again — Gladys was too ill to look after her son, but she was overjoyed that he'd survived the disaster.

Back at Port aux Basques, people waited anxiously for

their local boats to return with survivors. At 10 p.m., there was a call from the nearby community of Grand Bay saying its schooners had arrived with two bodies — one male, one female. Soon, other reports were coming in. One vessel from Isle aux Morte arrived with four bodies, three females and one male. Among them was Bridget Fitzpatrick, the only female crew member of the *Caribou*. Another body was identified as that of Nursing Sister Agnes Wilkie, the only Canadian nursing sister to die from enemy action in World War II.

Soon it became apparent to the people of Port aux Basques that their vessels would not be bringing back any survivors — only bodies. The buildings that had been made into temporary hospitals earlier that day were converted to temporary morgues to house the increasing number of dead.

As the extent of the tragedy became apparent to the people of Port aux Basques, confusion and uncertainty reigned. It wasn't clear to them why the escort vessel was taking the survivors to Sydney instead of their community, which was much closer. The confusion was later compounded by the lack of explanation from the officers and crew of the *Grandmere*, who were under navy orders to say nothing about the sinking of the *Caribou* or of their part in the rescue of the survivors. It was wartime, and the consensus among navy personnel was that "loose lips sink ships."

This secrecy, however, caused a number of rumours to circulate. Many people placed blame for the tragedy on the *Grandmere*, suggesting the minesweeper had not been sailing close enough to the *Caribou* at the time of the attack. Others insisted the *Grandmere* had left the disaster scene and returned to Sydney too early. Still others claimed the minesweeper had laid depth charges too close to survivors in the water.

Inquests into the tragedy met with the iron will of the navy and wartime orders that stated nothing was to be disclosed to the public. Questions such as whether or not a minesweeper was adequate protection for the *Caribou*, or why ferry crossings were conducted at night, were never satisfactorily answered.

There were, however, several changes made with respect to the issues that had bothered both Captain Taverner and Lieutenant Cuthbert as they had set out that night of October 13, 1942. After the sinking of the *Caribou*, the navy quietly recommended that there be no further night crossings on the Cabot Strait. It also went so far as to "recommend" to the owners of the ferries that all crew and passengers should wear their life belts throughout the crossing, and that lifeboat drills be held before setting sail. Moreover, Rear Admiral Leonard Murray, commander-in-chief of the Canadian Northwest Atlantic, informed his Newfoundland commander that in future, "an escort vessel escorting a single ship would afford more effective protection zigzagging 2,000 yards to 3,000 yards ahead..."

Those who survived that fateful night tried to live their lives to the fullest. For Gladys Shiers, getting on with her life proved to be difficult. Although the injuries she sustained from the blast finally healed and she gave birth to a healthy baby girl, her psychological bruises were slower to mend. For a long time after the sinking of the *Caribou*, she could not talk, and she suffered from terrifying nightmares. Over time, however, she began to recover, even overcoming her fear of the water so that she could give swimming lessons to her children. Her son Leonard was too young to be affected by the sinking, and his mother hardly ever spoke to him about it when he was growing up. He had no fear or phobia of water and in fact served in the navy for a period of time.

The tragedy of the *Caribou* was one of the most significant events of World War II for Atlantic Canadians, and Newfoundlanders in particular. It brought the war right to their doorstep, and never again did people in the vicinity take their security for granted. Today, a monument stands in Port aux Basques, a testament to the memory of the *Caribou* and all who did not survive that fateful night.

Chapter 8
The SS *Hungarian*

ears ago, many sections of coastline around the world were deathtraps because of their uncharted waters. Early mariners sailed in these sections, unaware that they hid sunken ledges, riptides, and places where the fog could blind them in minutes. Gradually, through the use of better sailing charts, careful surveys, and more efficient ways of marking troublesome areas, these spots became much less perilous.

Still, even with these improvements, there remain several dangerous areas that have earned reputations as marine graveyards due to the number of ships and lives that have been lost there. Cape Sable, on the southwesternmost point of Nova Scotia, is one of these areas.

The SS Hungarian

Until well into the 20th century, Cape Sable had the dubious distinction of being one of the worst places for shipwrecks along the Nova Scotia coast. The area is riddled with inlets, bays, small islands, and a series of underwater ledges. These ledges, which run parallel to the coast, are legendary and hide just under the waterline. Consisting of varying lengths and depths, they make navigating around Cape Sable treacherous because it is nearly impossible to tell the exact depth of the water at any given place — it may be shallow or fathoms deep within a short distance.

As if the ledges aren't enough to contend with, the currents and riptides sweeping up and down the Bay of Fundy, and the fog that permeates the coastline, make navigating all the more difficult. Throughout the 18th and 19th centuries, sailors tried to keep as far from the Cape Sable shore as possible to avoid succumbing to the hazards of the area. Nevertheless, countless vessels fell victim to them. Among these unfortunate ships was the SS *Hungarian*, a steamer owned by the prestigious Allan Line.

Built in 1859 in Dumbarton, Scotland, the SS *Hungarian* was employed as a passenger ship, but was also engaged as a Royal Mail carrier by the Canadian government. On February 8, 1860, she left Liverpool, England, for her regular transatlantic trip with a stopover in Queenstown, Ireland, to pick up more passengers and mail. On this particular voyage, the *Hungarian* was also carrying about one million dollars' worth of cargo — merchandise bound for stores in Quebec and Ontario.

The ship left Queenstown on February 9 and started out on her winter run. The *Hungarian* had two different routes — the summer route, which lasted from May to October and had the ship travelling between Liverpool and Quebec when the ice was gone from the St. Lawrence River, and the winter route, which lasted from November to April and took the ship from Liverpool, to Queenstown, to Portland, Maine.

The captain of the SS *Hungarian* was a well-liked man by the name of Thomas Jones. On the ship's inaugural winter run in November 1859, he and his crew had distinguished themselves by saving the lives of passengers and crew from the British schooner *Jean Martin*, which had been on the verge of sinking off the coast of Newfoundland during a severe winter storm. Though the effort had delayed the *Hungarian* by about six hours, the passengers of the steamer were extremely proud of their captain and crew and presented the rescuers with two golden sovereigns each. Arrangements were also made with a jeweller in London to have silver cups engraved for the heroes, to be presented at a later date.

Captain Jones and his crew were hoping for better weather on this run, but the gales on the Atlantic Ocean were frequent and intense in the winter of 1859–60. The *Hungarian* had already endured a severe storm on her last west-to-east crossing from Portland to Liverpool. A letter written by one of the passengers on that voyage was published in the February 4, 1860, issue of the *Liverpool Mercury*, just prior to the *Hungarian*'s departure on her tragic journey. In the letter, the writer, a reporter from New York, described the harrowing crossing and expressed his "heartfelt gratitude to one of the ablest and noblest captains that sail out of this or any other port in the world, Captain Jones, Steamship Hungarian, of the Canadian and Portland Line."

The west-to-east winter run for any transatlantic steamship was rarely as full as that of the summer run, but the east-to-west voyage usually carried quite a few immigrants. During the 1850s, and into the 1900s, most transatlantic trips leaving Europe and heading to North America carried immigrants coming west to start a new life. The *Hungarian*'s east-to-west voyage in the winter of 1860 was no different. By the time the final passengers for the trip had been picked up in Queenstown, there were close to 300 people on board, many of who were Irish immigrants.

Of the first class passengers aboard the *Hungarian* on this trip, quite a few were prominent citizens in their own communities. One man making the journey from Liverpool to Portland was a Canadian by the name of William Boultenhouse, who had gone to England on business and was now heading home to Sackville, New Brunswick. The son of Christopher Boultenhouse, a prominent shipbuilder, William was married with two children. Months earlier, he had sent a letter home describing his traumatic passage to Liverpool aboard the *Xiphias*, which had taken him to England from Saint John. The following is an excerpt from that letter:

For about a week after we left Saint John we experienced fine weather and a fair wind which increased to a hurricane and whilst running before it the ship broached to; in other words, the men at the wheel let her come up in the wind, as the sea was so heavy they could not steer her steadily — when she shipped a heavy sea, which hove her down until her yards were in the water. She did not right herself until the next day when we managed to get her before the wind again. Had she not been an exceeding strong ship she would never have got up again, but the fury of the sea still increased when she again broached to, which carried away jibboom head, foresail and top gallant mast and twisted her rudder head off, which was of oak, and finally made her unmanageable. We were in that helpless condition for three days and nights when we were taken off. I think we could not have been saved three hours after [we] were rescued as the gale still increased and we were nearly all exhausted.

Boultenhouse later wrote another letter from Liverpool, this one to his father. Dated January 30, 1860, it revealed the trepidation he was feeling toward his upcoming trip home aboard the *Hungarian*. The following is an excerpt:

The SS Hungarian

I almost dread coming home in the month of February but feel anxious to get home to my family after running such a narrow escape from a watery grave.

I often think of the Vanguard [a name that was interchangeable with the more classic Greek name "Xiphias"] and to consider that this is the first time I have crossed since then brings home thoughts as to how we should live for we know not what hour may be our last. It is awful work to cross the Atlantic in the winter season with a new ship as you do not know how she will work. Had the Xiphias not been very strong, she must surely have filled with water in a very short time — but I can only say that I am very thankful. I am here safe and well.

I hope to be home the last of February, if I am spared to do so ... My heart is full and tears are falling.

From your absent, but obedient and affectionate son, Wm. Boultenhouse.

Among the other first-class passengers on the *Hungarian* were Dr. Marino de Sama Diego and his wife, Amelia. The couple had met in London, where Dr. Sama Diego was undertaking medical studies. After a few months of courtship they married, and now they were about to start a new life in South America, where the doctor planned to set up a medical practice. The newlyweds had originally planned to sail aboard the *Persia*, a Cunard vessel, on January 26, but last minute details and drawn-out farewells had delayed them. Not wanting to wait too long for another ship to take them west, the Sama Diegos were pleased that they were able to obtain passage on the *Hungarian*.

Another married couple aboard the *Hungarian* were Robert Balmer and his wife, who were also travelling in first class. Balmer was employed as a buyer with A. Robertson & Company, a wholesale merchant company in Montreal. Every fall for the last eight years he'd travelled to Europe, returning home in the spring with the newest in fashions and merchandise for the company. He and his wife had originally planned to return on the SS *Bohemian*, but decided instead to sail on the *Hungarian* with Captain Jones, a man Balmer respected.

Also on board the ship were Marcus Talbot and his wife. Talbot, a politician, was born in Ireland and had immigrated to Canada only seven years earlier. He and his wife had just finished a holiday in Ireland and were returning to Canada West, where he would take up his duties as the Conservative member of the provincial parliament for East Middlesex.

There are no official records from the *Hungarian*'s fateful Atlantic crossing, so it is not known how the passengers or crew faired on this voyage. Were any of them ill, as was so often the case on transatlantic crossings? Did the first-class passengers spend their evenings in the grand salons of the ship, sipping wine and speculating about the war for Italian unification or the Hungarian Protestant revolt? How did the immigrants and other passengers in the steerage section spend their time? Did the children on board play hide-and-seek throughout the ship?

When news of the *Hungarian*'s demise first began to circulate, no one could understand how Captain Jones, a man with a great deal of experience sailing the Atlantic, had managed to get so close to Cape Sable's shore. Some suggested that part of the *Hungarian*'s steering mechanism must have been broken, while others speculated that her rudder was wrecked. Still other theorists insisted that Captain Jones had miscalculated his exact position in relation to the shoreline because of the storm that had blown in that day.

The only sure fact known about this disaster is that the *Hungarian* was wrecked about one and a half kilometres from shore on the infamous ledges of Cape Sable on the morning of February 20, 1860, some 12 days after leaving England.

At about 6 p.m. on February 19, the crew of a ship near Liverpool, Nova Scotia, noticed a vessel off the coast that appeared to be steering a course too close to shore to miss the ledges if she kept on her present heading. At three o'clock the next morning, a man from Cape Sable saw lights from a vessel that appeared to be moving in a northwesterly direction. By 4 a.m., word had spread that a ship might be in trouble. Fishermen, alerted to the possibility of a ship in distress, gathered along the shoreline, waiting to see if they could assist.

There was a terrible blizzard raging, and snow squalls made visibility difficult. People on shore would occasionally see a light in the distance, but then it would disappear again, obscured by the storm. As the sky lightened, it was soon evident that a large steamship had struck the ledges southwest of Cape Sable. All that could be seen were the mainmast, mizzenmast, and smokestack, as the breakers, whipped high by the February gale, crashed over the ship in a thundering roar.

The raging of the sea was taking its toll on the proud vessel; between the water crashing over her decks and the riptide pulling at her hull, the steamer did not stand a chance stranded on the ledges. With every surge of the waves, the great ship rolled heavily, and the freezing cold spray reached the top of her masthead. Eyewitnesses stated that the rigging of the mainmast was crowded with people, all of who were clinging desperately to the ropes. With the cold wind and icy spray from the breakers reaching high into the rigging, the people clinging there must have surely frozen before long.

Soon after sunrise, the force of the breakers breaching over the *Hungarian* caused the mainmast to crash overboard, and the smokestack began to lean forward as the bottom of the ship gave way. The mizzenmast was the last to go, with people still hanging on to its rigging. All the while, the fishermen on shore, who lived daily with the unpredictable ways of the ocean, watched in horror as the sea took its terrible toll.

Feeling helpless, they knew their boats would not be able to get through the wild surf. And, if by some miracle a boat *did* get through, it was doubtful there would be anyone on board the steamer to rescue.

The doomed ship began to break up, spilling her valuable cargo into the sea. Packages of goods from her upper decks were carried by the tide toward Baccaro Point. As soon as the tide turned, however, it started carrying everything that was washed from the wreck in the opposite direction.

The *Hungarian* had had six lifeboats on board, all of which had been used in the rescue of the *Jean Martin*'s passengers and crew earlier that winter. Only one lifeboat from the ship was found fully intact. It floated into Port La Tour, its bottom facing upwards with the oars still lashed to its sides. Bits and pieces of the other lifeboats were seen scattered about in the general area of the wreck.

By Tuesday, February 21, the storm had subsided and the snow squalls stopped altogether. People started out in search of goods to salvage, and soon there were many boats in the water, picking up whatever could be gathered. Bales of merchandise too large to be hauled aboard were broken open with axes, and the goods inside were transferred to the boats. Several bags of mail were found floating in the water, and these were handed over to local magistrates for safekeeping.

Meanwhile, barrels and trunks of clothing washed up on shore or were taken from the water. There were boxes of parasols, bales of cotton and silk, fancy hats, and other fine items. One box contained Moroccan wallets, while another held an ivory carved crucifix and other ornaments for use in a Catholic church.

Only two bodies from the *Hungarian* were found that Tuesday — that of a man and a little girl. The man, who was assumed to be a fireman from the steamer (judging by his manner of clothing), was found at Shag Harbour. The little girl was estimated to be less than two years of age and was found naked, washed up on the shore at Stony Island.

As time passed and only a few more bodies were discovered, people began to wonder what had happened to the rest of the ship's passengers. After one month, only six bodies had been recovered from the wreck. The sea gave up its seventh victim shortly thereafter. Then, in early April, a diver by the name of Sheridan found more bodies "entangled in the wreck alongside and in the gullies close by." In an interview with the *Halifax Journal*, Sheridan claimed to have also found bodies in amongst the cargo in the cargo hold, all tangled together, and reported that the ship's cabin doors were all closed, likely hiding more victims in the rooms beyond.

For the families of those who died that night on the *Hungarian*, there was the hopeful wish that their son, daughter, husband, or wife had missed getting to the vessel in time and was perhaps coming home on another ship. Hope soon turned to despair, though, as the shipping agents released some of the passengers' names. The purser's list from the

The SS Hungarian

Hungarian was forever lost, so the exact number of people on board is not known.

When Christopher Boultenhouse of Sackville learned of the fate of the *Hungarian* and heard there were no survivors, he recalled his son William's last letter and the sense of foreboding it had conveyed. To have William narrowly escape disaster aboard the *Xiphias* on his journey to Europe and then die so close to home aboard the *Hungarian* was especially heartbreaking for the elder Boultenhouse. On March 1, 1860, the following advertisement was placed in *The Yarmouth Herald*:

Information Wanted
Respecting the body or effects of Mr. William Boultenhouse a passenger in the late Steamer Hungarian, lately wrecked near Cape Sable:
Said Wm. Boltenhouse wore a ring with a green stone open for a likeness had a scar on his left cheek and thumb. Had light hair and was about thirty years of age. Any person finding this body or any papers or other effects belonging to deceased will please communicate the intelligence or forward such effects to the subscriber at Yarmouth, or, if more convenient, such effects may be forwarded to Halifax, to be sent on to his Father, Christopher Boultenhouse at Sackville, N.B. Any expenses incurred will be cheerfully paid by W.H. Gridley.

Bounty hunters figured there would be a reward for such a recovery since Christopher Boultenhouse was a very prominent shipbuilder. In fact, a hatbox belonging to William Boultenhouse had already been recovered. Then, on August 9, 1860, the *Hungarian* finally gave up his body. Dennis Horton, the president of the company that now owned the wreck, sent off the following telegram to Alexander Lawson, publisher of the *Yarmouth Herald*: "The body of Mr. Boultenhouse has been taken from the wreck of the Hungarian. On it, gold watch, ten pounds ten shillings in gold with papers."

Christopher Boultenhouse was one of the lucky ones. His son's body had been recovered and would rest in the family plot in Sackville. But hundreds of other families never got the chance to bury their lost loved ones.

For the people of Cape Sable and nearby fishing villages, the demise of the steamship *Hungarian* was a tale that was told over and over again. The date of the wreck was so imprinted on people's minds that it became a timeline from which to measure events — "About 50 years after the wreck of the steamer *Hungarian*..."

Because no one on board survived to explain why the ship was sailing so close to the shore, the reasons for the wreck of the SS *Hungarian* will forever remain a mystery. For the loved ones of those lost, this mystery only served to deepen the tragedy.

Chapter 9
The Countess
of Dufferin

Over the years, countless sailors and captains have risked their safety to help shipmates whose lives are threatened at sea. This is the story of one such heroic rescue, and of the ability of human beings to persevere — even when all hope seems to be gone.

In December 1891, the Yarmouth, Nova Scotia barque *Arlington*, a square-rigged vessel of some 849 tons, was finally headed to New York from Cardiff, Wales, in ballast. Leaving Cardiff had not been easy. Shortly before the *Arlington* was set to depart, members of the Cardiff Board of Trade had inspected her and concluded that she wasn't up to safety standards. The vessel had most of the necessary safety gear, but with winter fast approaching, the chances of the barque getting caught in a storm were very likely, and the board of trade felt that the ship's owners needed to be proactive. After some deliberation, members of the board demanded that the *Arlington* be outfitted with a new lifeboat, one of the newest design and build, before she left port. The owners of the ship, eager to get their vessel to New York, did as they were told. Once the lifeboat was purchased and loaded on board, the ship was allowed to leave.

All was going well for the *Arlington* on the journey back to New York. The vessel was running efficiently, even with the winter storm that had begun to brew. On the evening of December 28, however, the ship's master, Captain Samuel B. Davis, had a dream. This was no ordinary dream. Davis, a tough old captain from Yarmouth with 40 years' sailing experience, saw a square-rigged vessel, much like his own ship, in great distress, and could hear someone calling for help. The dream was so real that the captain jumped from his bed and raced to the deck to see what was happening. But when he looked out on the water, he saw no sign of trouble — except for the wild weather that was wreaking havoc on the *Arlington*'s reduced sails.

Still, Captain Davis couldn't dismiss the cry for help that he'd heard while slumbering — it had been so real. He also couldn't disregard the coordinates that kept playing back in his mind, coordinates that had been given in the same dream: "Lat. 52°30' N, Long. 21°20' W."

Once he was back in his quarters, the captain got out

his charts and determined the position of the coordinates. By his calculations, the *Arlington* was a day's sail away from the northward location that kept repeating itself in his head. The position was well off course of any steamers or sailing ships, and to veer off from his own set course would mean a great loss of time and money. But none of this seemed to matter. Unable to dismiss the cry for help or the sight of the suffering ship, Captain Davis gave orders to change the course of the *Arlington* and head toward the spot that marked 52°30' north latitude and 21°20' west longitude.

The next morning, Davis informed his first mate, James Hemeon, about the change in direction. Like the captain, Hemeon was a no-nonsense sailor from Yarmouth. When Davis explained to Hemeon that he'd altered the *Arlington's* course because of a dream, the first mate did not criticize the captain or scoff. He did, however, wonder if Davis had taken a bump on the head, because to deviate off course on a wild goose chase was certainly not something the captain would normally have done.

The first mate's concern grew deeper when Davis mentioned that his dream had also shown Hemeon himself rescuing crew members on the doomed vessel. As first mate, Hemeon was required to stay on board the *Arlington* during a rescue mission in case anything were to happen to the captain. But now Davis was suggesting that Hemeon would soon be flouting the rules and leaving his post to help rescue a potentially non-existent ship that was floundering in the middle of a winter storm.

Despite his misgivings, Hemeon followed the captain's orders to keep the *Arlington* heading northward. The first mate worried all day as the ship sailed farther and farther off course, and farther from New York.

Meanwhile, the *Countess of Dufferin*, a 542-ton barque built in Quebec and operated by the McCorkell Line out of Ireland, was in serious trouble. Earlier that month, she had been docked at Saint John, New Brunswick, where she was loaded with a cargo of lumber headed for Londonderry. Stevedores had filled her hold with fragrant spruce and pine from the forests of New Brunswick. Then, once her hold was full, they'd loaded more lumber onto her decks, securing it with chains to keep it from sliding around in the harsh winter weather of the North Atlantic.

The *Countess of Dufferin* left Saint John for Ireland on December 15. Captain Doble was in charge on this voyage, and, because the ship's home port was Londonderry, his crew consisted mainly of Irishmen.

The first 10 days of the voyage went well, but when Christmas Day rolled around, the crew awoke to a south-westerly gale that was pushing the ship along at a very fast pace. Captain Doble noticed that the barometer was falling steadily and sensed that they were in for some very heavy weather. He gave orders to "goose-wing" the main topsail so that its bottom was tied up tight and only a small portion of its top was actually left showing. Once this was done, the crew dropped the vessel's sea anchor to keep her headed into the wind and then waited for the storm they knew was coming.

They didn't have long to wait. In no time, hurricane-force winds came racing out of the north, smashing at the barque. The crew was terrified as they watched angry waves crash against the ship from all sides and wash over the cargo on deck. This cargo soon became water-logged, and the men realized that the ship didn't stand a chance in the horrific storm unless they got rid of the sodden lumber. They worked feverishly through the blinding rain and violent wind, trying to undo the chains that bound the cargo to the deck. More than once the men found themselves losing their footing and nearly getting washed overboard or crushed beneath the weight of the cargo. Finally, helped along by another wave, they managed to get the last piece of wood jettisoned over the side, and the deck was cleared.

Removing the weight of the deck cargo helped to stabilize the ship, but she continued to bob like a cork, pushed around by the wind. The seas were so heavy that it was difficult for crew members to keep their balance. Throughout Christmas Day, the winter storm beat at the vessel, putting great strains on a ship that had little to offer in the way of resistance to the weather.

By the next morning, the waves had smashed through the forward part of the ship's cabin, washing most of the food supply overboard. Worse, the lower hold was leaking badly and, because this was where the drinking water was stored, the crew was now without food *and* water. Captain Doble knew that unless the storm subsided, they would be in real trouble. Without food and water, it would only be a matter of time before the crew was unable to man the ship.

As the terrible weather continued, the oakum that was packed between the *Countess of Dufferin*'s planks started to give way, and more sea water rushed in. Captain Doble ordered his men to man the pumps, hoping to buy a little more time. But the water was coming in faster than they could pump it out.

The decks were icy with salt spray, the crew was exhausted, and the chances that one of the men would slip and fall overboard were mounting by the minute. Concerned about the safety of his crew, the captain ordered the pumping stopped. With that, there was nothing they could do but watch as the water grew higher and higher in the cargo hold and the *Countess of Dufferin* settled down into the waves. Soon, her decks were flush with the ocean.

For the next three days, Captain Doble and his crew huddled in the only shelter left on the ship — the forecastle. Freezing and starving, they stood by as the *Countess of Dufferin* held her own against the storm. The wood that had been packed so tightly in her hold at the beginning of her voyage helped to keep the ship floating for a while, but it soon began to swell. The crew knew it was only a matter of time before the vessel would literally be forced apart at the seams by the pressure of the swelling cargo.

While the men of the *Countess of Dufferin* were growing more and more disheartened, Captain Davis was keeping the *Arlington* on her new course. By December 29, the *Arlington's* first mate, along with the rest of her crew, were extremely worried. The storm they had encountered on their way north had been very strong, and if there really was a vessel in turmoil nearby, there was little chance that it would have weathered such forceful winds.

Captain Davis took the middle watch that night, and at around 3 a.m. he noticed a darker shape in the water. It appeared to be a ship. Adjusting his course in order to avoid a collision, the captain was angry that the ship had no running lights — the law required that all vessels show lights at night to prevent collisions.

Using a speaking trumpet, Davis hailed the crew of the other vessel and demanded to know why their ship had no lights. He was told that the darkened ship was the barque *Countess of Dufferin,* and that she was water-logged and sinking. Davis quickly realized that this was the ship in his dream.

Meanwhile, the men on the *Countess of Dufferin* were given a new sense of hope. They'd been blown so far off course by the storm that none of them had thought they'd be rescued. The men had all expected to go down with the ship. Now, the thought that they might actually be saved gave them the strength to hold on.

The whole crew of the *Arlington* was soon on deck as their ship made short tacks to keep close to the sinking vessel. At daybreak, Captain Davis called for volunteers to man the new lifeboat. Three able seamen — Frank Sullivan, Daniel Keefe, and Thomas O'Leary — stepped forward. The *Arlington*'s second mate, John Anderson, was preparing to get in the boat when the sea shifted and he was crushed between the lifeboat and the davits. He suffered three broken ribs and a broken arm, and, as a result, First Mate James Hemeon had to go in his place — just as Captain Davis had seen in his dream.

The seas were still churning when the lifeboat set out from the *Arlington* to rescue Captain Doble and his crew. Fighting the wind and waves with every stroke of the oar, the four men in the lifeboat pitted their skills against the elements. As they moved shakily toward the *Countess of Dufferin*, they were grateful to be in a new lifeboat and silently thanked the members of the Cardiff Board of Trade for insisting it be purchased. Had they been forced to go in one of the *Arlington*'s older boats, they surely would have capsized.

Even with the new boat, getting to the sinking ship proved to be very difficult because of the storm. But as the rescue crew got closer to the *Countess of Dufferin*, they realized that the bigger challenge would be getting the 11 men off the vessel without letting the wild waves smash the lifeboat against the ship. Struggling to keep their balance in the churning waters, the rescuers managed to secure a line to the forecastle and were soon taking the weakest of the *Countess of Dufferin* crew back to the *Arlington*.

Transferring the crew to the *Arlington* also proved to be difficult. Weak from lack of food and water, and suffering from frostbite, the exhausted survivors could barely help themselves. Consequently, it was up to the crew of the lifeboat to push and pull the men to safety.

It took over an hour and a half and two trips to the sinking ship before everyone was safe aboard the *Arlington*. The crew of the *Countess of Dufferin* was given food, medicine, and dry clothing. Some of the men were suffering greatly from frostbite and hypothermia, including Captain Doble, who was later hospitalized for two weeks.

After the heroic rescue of the captain and crew of the *Countess of Dufferin*, Captain Davis ordered a new course that would put the *Arlington* back on track to New York. On January 7, 1892, as they got closer to the shipping lanes, they hailed the steamer *Yesso*, which was bound for Baltimore. Soon, Captain Doble and his crew were transferred to the steamer and on their way to hospital.

Once he had recovered from his injuries, Captain Doble wrote a long thank you letter to Captain Davis. For his heroism, Davis was also awarded a gold watch, while Board of Trade Sea Gallantry medals were handed out to those who had manned the lifeboat that day. First Mate James Hemeon received a silver medal, and Able Seamen Daniel Keefe, Frank Sullivan, and Thomas O'Leary received bronze medals.

Captain Davis never offered an explanation for the dream that had led him and his crew to the *Countess of Dufferin*, but the watch he received is showcased in Yarmouth at a shop called "Samuel B's," which is owned by his descendants.

Further Reading

Dearborn, Dorothy. N*ew Brunswick Sea Stories: Phantom Ships and Pirate's Gold; Shipwrecks and Iron Men.* Saint John, NB: Neptune Publishing, 1998.

Galgay, Frank, and Michael McCarthy. *A Sea of Mother's Tears: Sea Stories from Atlantic Canada.* St. John's, NL: Flanker Press, 2003.

Graham, Mowry. *The Fastest Ship in the World.* Saint John, NB: READ Saint John, 1988.

How, Douglas. *Night of the Caribou.* Hantsport, NS: Lancelot Press, 1988.

MacMechan, Archibald. *Tales of the Sea.* Toronto, ON: McClelland & Stewart Limited, 1947.

Marsters, Roger. *Shipwreck Treasures: Disaster and Discovery on Canada's East Coast.* Halifax, NS: Formac Publishing, 2002.

Parsons, Robert C. *In Peril on the Sea — Nova Scotian Shipwrecks.* Halifax, NS: Pottersfield Press, 2000.

Parsons, Robert C. *Lost at Sea.* St. John's, NL: Creative Publishers, 1991.

Parsons, Robert C. T*he Edge of Yesterday: Sea Disasters of Nova Scotia.* Halifax, NS: Pottersfield Press, 1999.

Thurston, Arthur. *The Wreck of the Hungarian.* Yarmouth, NS: Arthur Thurston Publications, 1991.

Acknowledgments

Researching history has always been a part of my life, and I've met some wonderful researchers and writers while delving into the history of shipwrecks along Canada's eastern coastline. I'd like to acknowledge the work of William Thompson and the librarians at the Saint John Regional Library for their assistance with the numerous research questions. Also thanks to Faye Marks and the Quaco Museum staff in St. Martins, New Brunswick, for the answers to obscure questions, and to Kim Lalonde in Nova Scotia for graciously sharing her research on the SS *Hungarian*. Thanks also to John D. Stevenson of the Scottish Maritime History Research Centre in Edinburgh for going above and beyond with help in my research. To all those writers, journalists, and researchers who took time out to answer questions and point me in the right direction, thanks for being there when I needed you.

To my sons, André and Stefan, thanks for understanding when deadlines scrambled our family plans. Thanks also to my family and friends and fellow TAWG writers for their encouragement and support in writing this book. Appreciation and thanks to Sheree King Gilchrist and Declan Campbell in Dublin, Ireland, for their continued support.

And, finally, to my wonderful editor Jill Foran, whose comments have turned this manuscript into a reality that makes me proud. I couldn't have done this without you — thank you from the bottom of my heart.

About the Author

Carmel Vivier is an author and journalist living near Saint John, New Brunswick. Her writing, which has been published in magazines in Canada and the United States, covers topics in a number of fields, including history, business, law, photojournalism, and travel and tourism — to mention a few. She is an avid photographer and loves to travel, hike, and sail.

TRUE CANADIAN
AMAZING STORIES®

PIRATES AND PRIVATEERS

Swashbuckling Stories from the East Coast

Special 100ᵗʰ book
COLLECTOR'S EDITION

HISTORY
by Joyce Glasner

PIRATES AND PRIVATEERS
Swashbuckling Stories
from the East Coast

"The Truth out at last — Awful Disclosures!
Mutiny and Horrible Murders on the High Seas!!!"
A headline in The Morning Post June 10, 1844

Murder, mutiny, and mayhem were the order of
the day in the seas off the East Coast during the
golden age of sailing. Pillagers and opportunists
plied the ocean in search of riches in the holds of
American ships. And they invariably found what
they were looking for...

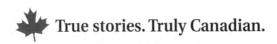 True stories. Truly Canadian.

ISBN 1-55439-013-3

CONVOYS OF WORLD WAR II
Dangerous Missions on the North Atlantic

"An ear-splitting explosion accompanied the torpedoes that hit...the Empire Gold. ...[It] immediately broke in two. The tanker's cargo of 10,000 tons of white spirit, as well as its own fuel, spewed onto the ocean. 'The flames just went sky high.'"

Nine men tell their personal stories of life at sea during World War II. In extreme danger, they battled seasickness, injury, and less than comfortable living conditions while avoiding floating mines and torpedoes in their efforts to guide ships safely across the Atlantic Ocean.

 True stories. Truly Canadian.

ISBN 1-55439-002-8

TRUE CANADIAN
AMAZING STORIES™

RESCUES ON THE HIGH SEAS

Tales of Survival, Hope, and Bravery

ADVENTURE
by Mark Chatham

RESCUES ON THE HIGH SEAS
Tales of Survival, Hope, and Bravery

"With every smash of a wave, the crack appeared almost to breathe, expanding to a five-centimetre gap that allowed water to shoot three metres into the compartment."

A wild and stormy ocean is not a friendly place to be, but for some this is their place of work. In extreme conditions, waves larger than houses can rip oil rigs apart and send them to the bottom of the ocean leaving survivors in desperate need. The response of search and rescue teams in times of danger is marked by courage and fierce determination. And it results in some terrifying stories.

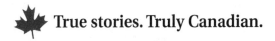 True stories. Truly Canadian.

ISBN 1-55439-003-6

AMAZING STORIES™

THE HALIFAX EXPLOSION

Surviving the Blast that Shook a Nation

HISTORY/HUMAN INTEREST

by Joyce Glasner

THE HALIFAX EXPLOSION
Surviving the Blast that Shook a Nation

*"Suddenly, a terrible blast jolted Andrew Cobb
out of his reverie. It felt as though a giant
hand had smacked the train, tipping it up
at a precarious angle before dropping
it back to the tracks with a crash."*

A boat full of explosives heads in to the harbour
as a large cargo ship steams out to sea. What happened next, on a fateful day in December 1917, is
etched in history. At least 1900 people lost their
lives and 9000 were injured when the largest
man-made explosion ever experienced ripped
through Halifax and nearby Dartmouth. Panic
reigned as the survivors struggled to compre-
hend what had happened.

 True stories. Truly Canadian.

ISBN 1-55153-942-X

OTHER AMAZING STORIES

These titles are available wherever you buy books. If you have trouble finding the book you want, call the Altitude order desk at **1-800-957-6888**, e-mail your request to: **orderdesk@altitudepublishing.com** or visit our Web site at **www.amazingstories.ca**

New **AMAZING STORIES** titles are published every month.